JAMES IREDELL
1790-99

THOMAS JOHNSON
1792-93

WILLIAM PATERSON
1793-1806

SAMUEL CHASE
1796-1811

OLIVER ELLSWORTH°
1796-1800

THOMAS TODD
1807-26

GABRIEL DUVALL
1811-35

JOSEPH STORY
1812-45

SMITH THOMPSON
1823-43

ROBERT TRIMBLE
1826-28

JOHN CATRON
1837-65

JOHN McKINLEY
1838-52

PETER VIVIAN DANIEL
1842-60

SAMUEL NELSON
1845-72

LEVI WOODBURY
1845-51

SAMUEL F. MILLER
1862-90

DAVID DAVIS
1862-77

STEPHEN J. FIELD
1863-97

SALMON P. CHASE°
1864-73

WILLIAM STRONG
1870-80

*member of today's Court is a direct descendant
of a former Justice—John Marshall Harlan
(page 144), namesake of his grandfather. Three
Justices served a record 34 years: John Marshall
(left, second row), Stephen J. Field (above,
fourth row), and John M. Harlan (far right).
Associate Justice Abe Fortas (pages 11, 138-9), is
the 95th Justice and President Lyndon B. Johnson's
first appointee to the Court.*

MORRISON R. WAITE°
1874-88

JOHN M. HARLAN
1877-1911

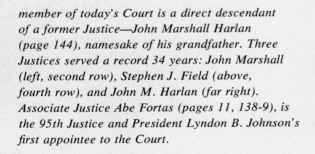

EQUAL JUSTICE
UNDER LAW

THE SUPREME COURT
IN AMERICAN LIFE

THE FOUNDATION OF
THE FEDERAL BAR ASSOCIATION

with the cooperation of the National Geographic Society

WASHINGTON, D. C.

SYMBOL OF POWER *and high authority,
the American eagle dominates the Seal
of the Supreme Court of the United
States. Justices ordered the emblem at
the third meeting of the Court, on
February 3, 1790. Designers adapted the
emblem from the Great Seal of the
United States. The streaming ribbon in
the eagle's beak carries the motto,* E
Pluribus Unum. *The Clerk of the Court
affixes the Seal to official papers such as
judgments, mandates, and writs.*

CONTENTS

Foreword

REVERED AND ABUSED as no other court has ever been, least known of the great institutions of the United States, the Supreme Court holds a unique power in the American system of government—a unique place in the American story.

To tell that story and to explain that power, the Foundation of the Federal Bar Association is publishing this book.

George Washington said that "the due administration of justice is the firmest pillar of good Government." The Foundation works to improve that administration, particularly in the federal courts. It acts for the Federal Bar Association, whose 12,400 members have served or now serve as attorneys or judges for the national government.

Believing that each citizen must be the final judge of good government, it has planned this book to serve the public.

When the First Congress was debating a bill to establish a federal court system, one Representative from New Hampshire expected it to "give great disgust." He could see no reason for a national judiciary, "unless it be to plague mankind." His fears have not materialized.

Most people never enter the federal courts, either as parties to a lawsuit or members of a jury—not even as spectators. They think of the courts as strange and remote if they think of them at all. And they believe, with some validity, that the law is a bramblepatch of technicalities and strange words. They might reasonably expect the Supreme Court to be the most remote of all, far from everyday affairs. And yet it is not; it is "supreme," but still very close to the lives and activities of all Americans.

From day to day the headlines announce its decisions, the editorials praise and denounce them, and citizens wrangle about them in town meetings, law schools, and living rooms.

We hope this story of the Court will be part of that debate, which began almost as soon as the Justices began to hear cases. Although we believe lawyers will enjoy it, it is not written especially for them, and legal technicalities are not its theme.

The theme is a national adventure. Its episodes are crises and struggles and conflicts. Its setting is a continent and beyond —and a few small rooms.

As our first edition went to press, we remembered that its setting is a world concerned for order and peace, when we learned that President Johnson had appointed Mr. Justice Goldberg as Ambassador to the United Nations. Now we introduce the 95th Judge to serve at the Supreme Court: Mr. Justice Abe Fortas.

To present this story, Dr. Melville Bell Grosvenor, President and Editor, and Dr. Melvin M. Payne, Executive Vice President and Secretary, have generously shared the resources of the National Geographic Society with the Foundation; and we are happy to thank them for their help. In this project, they and their staff colleagues have performed a great service to the Nation. We were privileged to work with these dedicated men and women of the National Geographic Society.

Members of our Foundation have selected landmark cases and reviewed both text and pictures which follow. The Foundation assumes full responsibility for the contents of the volume, which we are proud to sponsor.

For everyone who has worked on this book and for everyone who reads it, we hope it will mean a new devotion to the ideals of the Constitution, to the purposes which have been the special trust of the Supreme Court—"to form a more perfect Union, establish Justice . . . and secure the Blessings of Liberty to ourselves and our Posterity." And we hope it will mean a new pride in law as our way of using freedom.

EARL W. KINTNER
President, The Foundation
of the Federal Bar Association

The Supreme Court of the United States in Washington, D.C. —

A Heritage
of Law

"WE ARE very quiet there, but it is the quiet of a storm centre...." In these words Associate Justice Oliver Wendell Holmes—the Great Dissenter —described the Supreme Court of the United States in 1913. His words are just as true today. During its 175 years the winds of controversy have often swirled about the Court, its place in American government, and the 95 Justices who have made its decisions since the early days of the Republic.

"The Republic endures and this is the symbol of its faith."

Every system of justice has some kind of highest tribunal, some court of last resort, to give the final word on a case. But the Court gives the final word on a law, or on the powers of government under law, by the standards of the Constitution. Judicial review, scholars call it. Today some nations follow the American example, but when the Supreme Court developed this power it gave the world a new invention.

How the Court established this power in unlikely circumstances, how it has kept and used it, is the story of this book.

The men who gave us the Constitution and the Court began their work with a successful revolution. Captain Levi Preston fought at Lexington in 1775; he explained why 62 years later: "...what we meant in going for those red-coats was this: we always had governed ourselves, and we always meant to. They didn't mean we should."

In general, our legal tradition grows out

of the English tradition. But no English judge can say from the bench, as an American judge may say: "The law on the books says thus-and-so; but in spite of the fact that the legislature passed it in due form, this law is void—it is unconstitutional and therefore no law at all."

The English constitution has remained unwritten; it was, and still is, a mass of precedents, and of rules drawn from them. But in America the colonists got used to something else: the idea of one *written* agreement as the basis of government. In 1606 a charter from King James I outlined a plan of government for settlers in Virginia. Before the Pilgrims landed in 1620, they drew up the Mayflower Compact for themselves, with a solemn promise to make and obey "just and equal Laws" for the general good. Royal and proprietary colonies alike had their written charters.

THE COLONISTS came to think of these documents as sharing the sanctity of natural law, the supremacy of natural rights, the solidarity of human society. They were thinking of their charters as we think of our Constitution. Increasingly, many colonists came to regard Parliament's laws on colonial affairs as unjust, even tyrannical. They appealed to the principles of a higher law, which could nullify even Acts of Parliament. Finally, they appealed to arms—they fought the Revolution.

War brought victory; peace brought trouble. America's first constitution, the "Articles of Confederation and perpetual Union," set up a "firm league of friendship," a government so simple it didn't work. Each state kept its "sovereignty, freedom and independence," and every power not expressly given to Congress. That Congress, one house in which each state had one vote, had to rely on the states for soldiers or money or law enforcement. Often the states didn't cooperate.

Distressed, George Washington saw that the country had "thirteen heads, or one head without competent powers." John Jay warned in 1783 that Europe watched "with jealousy, and jealousy is seldom idle"—weakness at home might tempt assault from abroad. The states squabbled among themselves over trade; in 1786 James Madison wrote gloomily to Thomas Jefferson about the "present anarchy of our commerce." Protests grew sharper, until Congress reluctantly called for a convention to meet in Philadelphia in May, 1787, "for the sole and express purpose of revising the Articles of Confederation."

The delegates straggled in, elected Washington to preside, and with great courage and good sense disobeyed their instructions. They went to work to create a new government—"a *national* government . . . consisting of a *supreme* Legislative, Executive and Judiciary." Their splendid disobedience produced the Constitution of the United States. It was not the Articles they revised, it was the future.

They invented something new, a plan for power the world had never seen before, an intricate system with both the states and the central government dealing directly with the people.

After long angry debates they compromised on a new kind of Congress, with two houses. After more wrangles they accepted the idea of an executive, a President. Without any argument at all the delegates

"THE LAW, WHEREIN, AS IN A MAGIC MIRROR, *we see reflected not only our own lives,*" noted Oliver Wendell Holmes, Jr., "*but the lives of all men that have been!*" *Visitors stand at the threshold of the Nation's citadel of law, the Supreme Court. The Dome of the Capitol rises in the west.*

9

accepted the proposal for a Supreme Court. They agreed on the kinds of cases courts of the United States should try; when they disagreed over details for the lower courts, they left the matter up to the new Congress.

Soberly, for a long time, they thought about the most important problem of all. The country's simple government under the Articles had not worked well. Now the delegates were offering a complicated arrangement with many more points to quarrel about—who should make the final decision in disputes about the Constitution?

TO THIS QUESTION the delegates gave no final answer. But they adopted a sentence to make an answer possible: "This Constitution, and the Laws of the United States which shall be made in Pursuance thereof... shall be the Supreme Law of the Land...."

Angry debates and even brawls accompanied the immediate question: Should the people accept this new system? Patrick Henry spoke the fears of many when he cried, "it squints towards monarchy. Your President may easily become King."

And where was a bill of rights? Most of the states had one in their own constitutions, and saw dangers in a document that failed to provide a list of liberties. Pamphlets came thick and fast. Some cried:

That the convention in great fury
Have taken away the trial by jury;
That liberty of press is gone,
We shall be hang'd, each mothers son....

For months the issue was uncertain, because nine of the original 13 states had to ratify the Constitution before it would become law. But by June 21, 1788, the ninth —New Hampshire—had acted.

In the First Congress, James Madison led in drafting amendments to protect the freedom and rights of the people; the states approved them promptly, and, by Decem-

ber 15, 1791, the Bill of Rights was in force.

Now a "more perfect Union" replaced the faltering "league of friendship," and the new nation began its great experiment of liberty under the law. In time, the Supreme Court became the interpreter of the supreme law of the land—not because the delegates provided that it must, but because things worked out that way.

Associate Justice William J. Brennan, Jr., says: "... the Founding Fathers knew better than to pin down their descendants too closely. Enduring principles rather than petty details were what they sought to write down. Thus it is that the Constitution does not take the form of a litany of specifics."

And so disputes over its meaning have continued. But Chief Justice John Marshall declared: "It is emphatically the province and duty of the judiciary department to say what the law is." He warned: "We must never forget that it is a *constitution* we are expounding ... intended to endure for ages to come, and consequently, to be adapted to the various *crises* of human affairs."

Charles Evans Hughes, who would become Chief Justice himself, stated the Court's responsibility more bluntly in 1907: "We are under a Constitution, but the Constitution is what the judges say it is."

So the Judges find its words "loaded," as Associate Justice Byron R. White says today. For more than a century the Court has been deciding cases that twine about a single statement, Congress shall have the power to regulate commerce among the several states. On four simple words, "due process of law," the Court has written volumes.

Still, in dealing with constitutional problems, the Court is free to change its mind. Justices have overruled their predecessors and themselves, to correct a decision in the light of experience. They sit as "a kind of Constitutional Convention in continuous session," said Woodrow Wilson. Their

RARE INFORMAL PORTRAIT *of the Justices shows members of the Court in the paneled and pilastered East Conference Room. They are (left to right) Associate Justices William J. Brennan, Jr., Potter Stewart, Byron R. White, Hugo L. Black, Abe Fortas, William O. Douglas, and John M. Harlan, Chief Justice Earl Warren, and Associate Justice Tom C. Clark. Bound by the propriety and dignity of their office, the Justices seldom grant permission for pictures of themselves in a casual pose. Rembrandt Peale's famous "porthole portrait" of Chief Justice John Marshall hangs above them.*

JOSEPH J. SCHERSCHEL, ROBERT S. OAKES, AND ARLAN R. WIKER © N.G.S.

changing views have helped make the Constitution meet the needs of each successive generation. But again and again they have stirred up wrath and controversy.

Before he became Associate Justice, Robert H. Jackson pointed out that Supreme Court Justices derive their offices from the favor of Presidential appointment and Senate confirmation. And they are "subject to an undefined, unlimited, and unreviewable Congressional power of impeachment. . . . Certainly so dependent an institution would excite no fears. . . ."

And yet, he said, "this Court has repeatedly overruled and thwarted both the Congress and the Executive. It has been in angry collision with the most dynamic and popular Presidents in our history. Jefferson retaliated with impeachment; Jackson denied [the Court's] authority; Abraham Lincoln disobeyed a writ of the Chief Justice; . . .

Wilson tried to liberalize its membership; and Franklin D. Roosevelt proposed to 'reorganize' it."

You feel this timeless epic when you stand in the empty Courtroom today. Here the voices of famous lawyers seem to come out of the stillness—John Quincy Adams, formidable and old; Henry Clay, taking a pinch from the Judges' snuffbox; Daniel Webster, in his legendary tribute to his alma mater, Dartmouth—"a small college, and yet there are those who love it."

Here is great drama—a Dred Scott case inflaming the passions of a nation. And an attorney, mortally ill, who left a hospital bed to address the Court, then mustered strength to write thanking the Justices for their courtesy before he died the next day.

Here is intense emotion—Justice James M. Wayne during the Civil War years speaking for the Union when his state and his

family disowned it. And a young lawyer standing wordless at three invitations to begin, finally managing to say, "Mr. Chief Justice, may I have a minute to compose myself? I'm scared to death."

Here are nine Judges whose Court is the arbiter of the American government—the umpire of the federal system. Their decisions represent a majority, if not all, of the members, but their awesome responsibility falls in the end on individual shoulders. As Associate Justice John Marshall Harlan explains today: "Under his oath, each member of the Court must decide each case as if he were its only judge."

Here, in the richness of its past, the strong and clashing forces it must meet, the mystery it must foresee, is the most sedate and yet most dramatic of all the elements of government. Here, in short, is the Supreme Court of the United States.

THUNDEROUS ORATOR, *lawyer Daniel Webster argued the Dartmouth College case before the Supreme Court and won a landmark decision that protected private property rights and encouraged growth of business corporations in all branches of commerce and industry.*

When the Justices decided this case, they were performing the continuing function of the Court—to interpret the Constitution and to define the law of the land.

Every citizen has been affected by opinions of the Court since the early days of the Republic. "It passes on his property, his reputation, his life, his all," said Chief Justice John Marshall, who heard the Dartmouth College case.

Residents of Hanover, New Hampshire, stroll before Dartmouth Hall in this 1803 drawing (above left). When the state tried to turn Dartmouth from a privately owned college into a state university, the college filed suit and retained Webster, whose argument became legend. "The question is simply this," he contended: "Shall our state legislature be allowed to take that which is not their own . . . ?" No, said the Supreme Court, when it held for the first time that a charter of incorporation is a contract which no state has constitutional power to impair.

At the Supreme Judicial Court of the United States, begun and held at New York (being the Seat of the National Government) on the first Monday of February, and on the first day of said month Anno [Domini] 1790.

Present.

The Honble. John Jay Esquire Chief Justice
The Honble. {William Cushing, and
James Wilson, Esqrs.} Associate Justices.

This being the day assigned by Law, for commencing the first Session of the Supreme Court of the United States, and a sufficient Number of the Justices not being now convened, the Court is adjourned by the Justices now present, untill to Morrow, at one of the Clock in the afternoone. —

Tuesday, February 2nd. 1790.

Present.

The Honble. John Jay Esqr. Chief Justice.
The Honble. {William Cushing
James Wilson, and
John Blair, Esqrs.} Associate Justices.

Proclam[ation]

Decisions for Liberty

WHENEVER JUDGES, lawyers, and legal scholars gather and the talk turns to the Constitution and the men who made it the law we live by, one name inevitably enters the conversation: John Marshall of Virginia.

"My gift of John Marshall to the people of the United States was the proudest act of my life," said John Adams, the second President, years after he left office.

Adams not only chose Marshall for Chief Justice in 1801, he forced a reluctant Senate to confirm the appointment. He had every right to be proud.

Marshall asserted the Court's mightiest power and dignity in its first great crisis. His decisions set the course for a bold venture —a new republic's voyage to greatness among the nations of the world. Those decisions, and many that followed, mirror the history of the Supreme Court and, indeed, of the Republic itself. At the Court today Justices and others still speak of Marshall as the "great Chief."

The Constitution called for a Supreme Court and a federal judiciary, but left it to Congress to spell out the details. Congress did so in the Judiciary Act of 1789. Connecticut's Oliver Ellsworth—later to serve four years as Chief Justice—led the drafting in committee. This law created 13 district courts, with one judge apiece, and three circuit courts, eastern, middle, southern. Above these it set the Supreme Court, with a Chief Justice and five Associates.

For the first Chief Justice, President Washington picked John Jay, New York-born statesman and diplomat. The President weighed sectional jealousies and personal ability in selecting Associate Justices —John Blair of Virginia, William Cushing of Massachusetts, James Wilson of Penn-

sylvania, James Iredell of North Carolina, and John Rutledge of South Carolina. All had helped establish the Constitution.

But only three of the Judges had reached New York, a temporary capital city, in 1790, when the Court convened for the first time. Required by law to sit twice a year, it began its first term with a crowded courtroom and an empty docket. Appeals from lower tribunals came slowly; for its first three years the Court had almost no business at all.

Spectators at early sessions admired "the elegance, gravity and neatness" of Justices' robes. But when Cushing walked along New York streets in the full-bottom professional wig of an English judge, little boys trailed after him, a sailor called, "My eye! What a wig!" Cushing never wore it again.

In 1791, the Court joined Congress and the President at Philadelphia; it heard discussions of lawyers' qualifications, but little else. Still, other duties exhausted the Justices. The Judiciary Act of 1789 required them to journey twice a year to distant parts of the country and preside over circuit courts. For decades they would grumble, and hope Congress would change this system; but Congress meant to keep them aware of local opinion and state law.

Stagecoaches jolted the Justices from city to city. Sometimes they spent 19 hours a day on the road. North of Boston and in the South, roads turned into trails. Justice Iredell, struggling around the Carolinas and Georgia on circuit, and hurrying to Philadelphia twice a year as well, led the life of a traveling postboy. Finding his duties "in a degree intolerable," Jay almost resigned. Congress relented a little in 1793; one circuit trip a year would be enough.

Sensitive issues appeared in some of the Court's first cases. Its decision in *Chisholm*

FIRST OFFICIAL MINUTES *of the Supreme Court of the United States contain an error— the word "Judicial." Authorities believe the Court's Clerk, a Massachusetts man, inserted the word because the highest tribunal in his state was the "Supreme Judicial Court." The National Archives in Washington, D. C., preserves the record.*

FIRST CHIEF JUSTICE, *John Jay opened the initial session of the Supreme Court on February 1, 1790. President George Washington had named the 43-year-old New York lawyer to head the highest tribunal in the land after Congress had set the number of Justices at six in 1789.*

"He was remarkable for strong reasoning powers, comprehensive views, indefatigable application, and uncommon firmness of mind," said one of Jay's friends. The Federalist statesman set lasting standards of judicial excellence during five years of service as Chief Justice. Jay's Court established an all-important precedent by refusing to advise the President on matters of law; to this day, the Court speaks only on specific cases that come before it for review.

At Washington's request, Jay, still Chief Justice, embarked upon a famous diplomatic mission to Great Britain in 1794 to settle quarrels over British troops in the Northwest and private debts to British creditors. The treaty that Jay negotiated preserved the peace when war might well have destroyed the new Nation.

Jay resigned as Chief Justice in 1795 and became Governor of New York, serving for two terms. His tenure on the bench launched a tradition of high-minded dignity that continues to distinguish the Supreme Court.

v. *Georgia* shocked the country. During the Revolution, Georgia had seized property from men loyal to the Crown. With a pre-Revolution claim on such an estate, two South Carolinians asked the Court to hear their suit against Georgia. It agreed, saying the Constitution gave it power to try such cases. But when the day for argument came in 1793, Georgia's lawyers did not appear. The Court gave its decision anyway, in favor of the South Carolinians.

Georgia raged; other states took alarm. They were trying to untangle finances still snarled from the war. If they had to pay old debts to "Tories" they might be ruined. They adopted the Eleventh Amendment, forbidding any federal court to try a lawsuit against a state by citizens of some other state. Thus the people overruled the Supreme Court for the first time, and established a far-reaching precedent of their own. They would give the ultimate decision on constitutional disputes.

War between Britain and France brought two more basic precedents. President Washington was working desperately to keep the United States neutral and safe; he sent the Court 29 questions on international law and treaties, and begged for advice. The Justices politely but flatly refused to help. Under the Constitution, they said, they could not share executive powers and duties, or issue advisory opinions.

To this day, the Supreme Court will not give advice; it speaks only on the specific cases that come before it.

But by its decision in *Glass* v. *Sloop Betsy,* in 1794, the Court did defend neutral rights and national dignity.

Defying the President's neutrality proclamation, French privateers were bringing captured ships into American ports. There French consuls decided if the ships were to be kept as lawful prize.

Betsy, Swedish-owned, had American cargo aboard when the French raider *Citizen Genet* caught her at sea and took her to Baltimore. Alexander S. Glass, owner of a share of the cargo, filed suit for his goods, but the district court in Maryland ruled that it could not even hear such cases.

With the prestige of the country at stake, the government quickly appealed to the

CUPOLA-CROWNED *Royal Exchange in New York City housed the first meeting of the Supreme Court. Justices deliberated on the second floor of the gambrel-roofed hall. A brick arcade shades the ground floor, an open-air market where Broad and Water Streets intersect. During the first term the Judges appointed a court crier and a clerk, and admitted lawyers to the bar, but heard no cases. After two sessions here, the Court reconvened in Philadelphia, the national capital until 1800.*

"UNCOMMONLY CROUDED," *reports the* New York Daily Advertiser *(right) of the scene at the Supreme Court's scheduled opening; curious spectators had to wait until the next day to see the Court formally convened. Widely reprinted, such accounts described the "novel experiment of a National Judiciary" for readers throughout the states. Last paragraph cites new location of the federal court that moved out of the Exchange to make room for the Justices.*

nd reading. Adjourned.

THE SUPREME COURT
Of the United States, convened yesterday in this city; but a sufficient number of the Judges not being present to form a quorum, the same was adjourned till this day one o'clock.

The Hon. John Jay, Chief Justice of the United States,

The Hon. William Cushing, and

The Hon. James Wilson, Assistant Justices, appeared on the bench.

John M'Kesson, Esq. acted as Clerk.

The Court Room at the Exchange was uncommonly crouded.—The Chief Justice and other Judges of the Supreme Court of this state; the Federal Judge for the District of New-York; the Mayor and Recorder of New-York; the Marshal of the district of New-York; the Sheriff, and many other officers, and a great number of the gentlemen of the bar attended on the occasion.

The Federal Court for the district of New-York will be opened this day, in the Consistory room opposite the Dutch Church in Garden-street.

BOSTON,
Plymouth & Sandwich
MAIL STAGE,

CONTINUES TO RUN AS FOLLOWS:

LEAVES Boston every Tuesday, Thursday, and Saturday mornings at 5 o'clock, breakfast at Leonard's, Scituate; dine at Bradford's, Plymouth; and arrive in Sandwich the same evening. Leaves Sandwich every Monday, Wednesday and Friday mornings; breakfast at Bradford's, Plymouth; dine at Leonard's, Scituate, and arrive in Boston the same evening.

Passing through Dorchester, Quincy, Wyemouth, Hingham, Scituate, Hanover, Pembroke, Duxbury, Kingston, Plymouth to Sandwich. *Fare*, from Boston to Scituate, 1 doll. 25 cts. From Boston to Plymouth, 2 dolls. 50 cts. From Boston to Sandwich, 3 dolls. 63 cts.

.N. B. Extra Carriages can be obtained of the proprietor's, at Boston and Plymouth, at short notice.— ☞STAGE BOOKS kept at Boyden's Market-square, Boston, and at Fessendon's, Plymouth.

LEONARD & WOODWARD.

BOSTON, *November* 24, 1810.

"**CIRCUITS PRESS HARD** *on us all,"
moaned Chief Justice John Jay. A 1789
Act of Congress, requiring Supreme
Court jurists to preside twice a year over
circuit courts scattered throughout the
Union, meant months of rugged travel.*

*Broadside (left) depicts common mode
of transportation. After jolting in a
stagecoach many hours daily over
savage roads of ruts and rocks or
helping lift the stagecoach from
quagmires of mud, the Justices passed
restless nights in crowded way stations
such as Fairview Inn on Frederick road
(above) near Baltimore, Maryland.*

*Battered and exhausted by the rigors
of travel, Judges often arrived at the
circuit courts too late or too sick to
hold a session. Still, their visits served
to acquaint the people with the new
judiciary branch.*

TATTERED *knee breeches of John Marshall, the Nation's fourth Chief Justice, reveal his lifelong habit of bedraggled dress. But his speech was always persuasive, his genial charm unfailing, in a courtroom or out of it. Here, at a Virginia tavern during his circuit-riding days, he holds dapper young lawyers spellbound for nearly an hour. One traveler said that to try to describe Marshall's eloquence "would be an attempt to paint the sunbeams." Injuries suffered in a stage-coach crash while on circuit hastened his death.*

19

Supreme Court. Not foreign consuls but federal courts would decide American claims, the Justices ruled. Europe heard this decision; and the United States became, as Washington hoped, "more respectable."

OLD DEBTS AND GRUDGES were troubling relations between the United States and Great Britain. President Washington sent Chief Justice Jay to London as a special minister to settle the quarrels, and Jay negotiated a treaty. When he returned New York elected him governor, and he resigned from the Court.

To succeed him Washington chose John Rutledge; the Senate rejected the nomination. Patrick Henry, now an old man, declined to serve, and Oliver Ellsworth became Chief Justice.

Jay's Treaty infuriated Americans who thought it too favorable to Britain. Feeling still ran high in 1796 as the Court reviewed the case of *Ware* v. *Hylton*. Many British subjects had claims against Americans from contracts made before the Revolution; some states had canceled these by law, but treaty provisions required their payment.

In his only argument before the Supreme Court, John Marshall defended a Virginia law abolishing payments to British creditors; he lost. A treaty of the United States must override the law of any state, ruled the Justices. When the Nation pledges its word, it must keep faith—and the Nation speaks with one voice, not with 13, not with 50.

But two raucous choruses were shouting abuse at each other when the Court met at Philadelphia for the last time, in August,

1800. The government was moving to a new site by the Potomac, where no one had even planned a judiciary building. In 1801 Congress loaned the Court a little ground-floor room in the unfinished Capitol; it crowded the Justices for seven years.

Changing capitals was easier than changing the government. With vast excitement, the people were tussling with an issue the Constitution ignored; painfully, nervously, they were working out a two-party system.

Against the Federalists, "the good, the wise, and the rich," the party of Washington and Adams, stood the admirers of Vice President Thomas Jefferson—"the Man of the People." Calling themselves Republicans, the Jeffersonians wanted to give the people more of a voice in government; they praised the ideals of the French Revolution, they had nothing but distrust for Britain.

During John Adams's term as President, the French insulted the administration from abroad and the Republicans criticized it at home. Federalists had run the new government from the first. They feared attacks on themselves as attacks on the new Constitution. Hearing French accents in every critical sentence, they passed the Sedition Act of 1798.

This law endangered anyone who spread "false, scandalous and malicious" words against the government or its officers, to "bring them . . . into contempt or disrepute." It would expire with Adams's term of office on March 3, 1801.

"Finding fault with men in office was already an old American custom," writes one historian; "indeed, it had become an

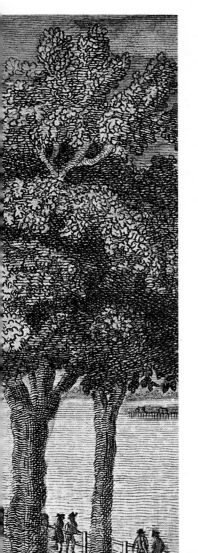

FRENCH FRIGATE L'Embuscade *sails past the Battery of New York City in this contemporary engraving. During President Washington's Administration, French raiders roamed off American coasts, seized merchant ships, and took them into port for French consuls to decide if they were lawful prize. This practice defied the authority of the United States and its right to maintain neutrality in the war between France and Britain. When the French privateer* Citizen Genet *(below left) captured a Swedish ship with American cargo, a federal district judge held that his court had no jurisdiction in the matter. By its 1794 decision in the case* **Glass** v. **Sloop Betsy,** *the Supreme Court declared that American courts would decide all cases within the American domain.*

essential part of the pursuit of happiness."

Supreme Court Justices presided at trials on circuit and sent Republican journalists to jail for sedition. But the Republicans kept on criticizing, and shouting "Tyranny!" The Federalists answered with furious cries of "Treason!"

In the 1800 elections the "Lock Jaw" Federalists were routed—"Mad Tom" Jefferson would be President, his followers would control Congress.

Gloomily, the Federalists hoped that judges could save the Constitution from these "radicals." Chief Justice Ellsworth was ailing; he resigned. Jay refused to serve again. So Adams gave his Secretary of State,

John Marshall, to the Supreme Court. In Congress, the lame-duck Federalists passed a law to reduce the Court's membership to five (one less Justice for a Republican President to name). Abolishing circuit duties for the Justices and providing other reforms, this law set up new circuit courts with 16 judges. Adams quickly made his appointments—the famous "Midnight Judges."

Enraged, one Republican from Kentucky called Adams's tactics "the last effort of the most wicked, insidious and turbulent faction that ever disgraced our political annals."

Jefferson took his oath of office on March 4, 1801. Without precedents and with passions running high, the Presidency and the

HOMES OF THE COURT: *Philadelphia's Independence Hall (left) sheltered the Judges for two days in 1791—all they needed for their February term. In August they met in Old City Hall (above, with cupola), which served them for a decade. Their first session in Washington, D. C., came in 1801.*

MEMENTOS OF JAY: *The Chief Justice, an avid student of astronomy, brought the celestial globe from England in 1795 after signing the Jay Treaty. His spectacles lie on a parchment-bound Latin book he used at Kings College, forerunner of Columbia University. He wrote his name on the title page. A Sèvres inkwell sits at right. The State of New York preserves these relics in the recently restored John Jay Homestead near Katonah, New York.*

Congress passed for the first time from one party to another. And some citizens were afraid that the judiciary was in mortal danger.

Soon after his Inauguration, Jefferson wrote that the Federalists had "retreated into the judiciary as a stronghold, the tenure of which renders it difficult to dislodge them."

But the Republicans repealed the lame-duck Judiciary Act, while horrified Federalists lamented, "the Constitution has received a wound it cannot long survive," and "the angels of destruction . . . are making haste."

Meanwhile, William Marbury of Washington went straight to the Supreme Court, looking for a commission as justice of the peace for the District of Columbia. Adams had appointed 42 such officials, the Senate frantically confirmed them, and Adams sat at his desk until late on his last night in office to sign their commissions. Then a messenger rushed the papers to the State Depart-

"**HILLS, VALLEYS,** *morasses and waters," said Thomas Jefferson of the site chosen for Washington, here depicted in 1800. Stone bridge (center) spans Rock Creek near Georgetown (left). In background at right rises Jenkins Hill, where the Capitol stands today. The Senate and the House shared the old North Wing (below), first structure of the Capitol, with the Supreme Court. Here the Justices met in various rooms from 1801 until 1935. During the early years when construction displaced the Judges, they had to meet in nearby homes.*

ment for Marshall, still acting as Secretary, to affix the great seal of the United States. In the confusion some of the commissions got lost, Marbury's among them.

In December, 1801, Marbury applied to the Court for a writ of mandamus ordering James Madison, the new Secretary of State, to give him his commission. The Court agreed to hear the case—a bold action, for rumor was saying the Justices "must fall" by impeachment. Then the Republican Congress passed a law stopping the Court's sessions for 14 months: another threat. When the Justices finally sat again in 1803, they heard argument in Marbury's case.

If the Court ordered Madison to produce that commission, he could simply ignore the order; President Jefferson would defend him. If the Court denied Marbury's right to his commission, Jefferson could claim a party victory. Either way the Court's prestige—and perhaps its members—must fall.

Marshall found an escape from this dilemma. He announced the decision on February 24, and proclaimed the most distinctive power of the Supreme Court, the power to declare an Act of Congress unconstitutional. Point by point he analyzed the case. Did Marbury have a legal right to his commission? Yes. Would a writ of mandamus enforce his right? Yes. Could the Court issue the writ? *No*.

Congress had said it could, in the Judiciary Act of 1789. It had given the Court an original jurisdiction in such cases—power to try them for the first time. But, said Marshall

25

triumphantly, the Constitution defined the Court's original jurisdiction and Congress could not change it by law. Therefore that section of the law was void.

The Court had issued such writs before, but Marshall ignored the fact. He declared for all time the supremacy of the Constitution over any conflicting law. Other judges had said as much, but Marshall added: "It is, emphatically, the province and duty of the judicial department, to say what the law is."

In renouncing a minor jurisdiction he asserted a great one, perhaps the greatest in the long annals of the law. The Supreme Court's power as interpreter of the Constitution rests on this precedent to this day.

A few days after the decision in *Marbury* v. *Madison,* the Court amazed the Jeffersonians again. They had passed a Judiciary Act of their own, restoring the Court's old membership and circuit duties. The Justices ruled that it was constitutional, and for a while talk of impeachment died down.

"OYEZ! OYEZ! OYEZ!...the grand inquest of the nation is exhibiting to the Senate...articles of impeachment against Samuel Chase, Associate Justice...." The Supreme Court was on trial; if Chase fell, Marshall might be next.

Feared as a "ringleader of mobs, a foul mouthed and inflaming son of discord" when he led the Sons of Liberty in 1765, Chase "was forever getting into some... unnecessary squabble" as a Judge 40 years later. He campaigned openly for Adams. On circuit he tried Republicans without mercy. In 1803 he told a Baltimore grand jury that "modern doctrines" of "equal liberty and equal rights" were sinking the Constitution "into a mobocracy, the worst of all popular governments."

His enemies saw their chance. The House of Representatives voted to bring him before the Senate for trial, charging that his partisan behavior—in and out of court—amounted to "high Crimes and Misdemeanors" under the Constitution.

Vice President Aaron Burr had arranged a special gallery for ladies when the "grand inquest" opened on February 4, 1805. Burr had killed Alexander Hamilton in a duel and New Jersey wanted him for murder; but

he presided sternly, rebuking Senators who were eating cake and apples. "We are indeed fallen on evil times," said one. "The high office of President is filled by an *infidel;* that of Vice-President by a *murderer.*"

Representative John Randolph of Roanoke, the brilliant, erratic Virginian, fought to prove Chase unfit for the Court. Luther Martin of Maryland, who could hold more law and more brandy than any other attorney of his time, led Chase's defense. Marshall and 51 other witnesses testified.

Amid "a vast concourse of people... and great solemnity," the Senators acquitted

ON HIS LAST NIGHT *in the White House, President John Adams (right) sat up signing official commissions for members of his party, the Federalists, defeated in the 1800 elections. But some of the papers got lost, including one to make William Marbury of Washington a justice of the peace. The victorious party of Thomas Jefferson, the Republicans, angrily called Adams's appointees "Midnight Judges"; political passion ran high when Marbury tried to claim his office by filing suit in the Supreme Court against James Madison, the new Secretary of State. Chief Justice John Marshall avoided an open clash with Congress and the President by ruling that the Court had no power to order Marbury's commission restored, although the Judiciary Act of 1789 said it did. The Court held that provision of the law null and void. Thus for the first time, in* **Marbury v. Madison,** *the Supreme Court exercised its power to declare an Act of Congress unconstitutional. This was not the first example of judicial review—the Court had upheld the validity of a federal law in 1796—but it remains the classic precedent for the Supreme Court's role as final interpreter of the Constitution.*

27

"**HIS BLACK EYES**... *possess an irradiating spirit, which proclaims the imperial powers of the mind that sits enthroned therein," a lawyer wrote of John Marshall, known as "the great Chief Justice." Named to the Court in 1801, Marshall presided for 34 years. The compelling force of his logic brought prestige to the judicial department. His far-sighted opinions, vitalizing the law to this day, helped mold the Nation by upholding the powers of the Union against claims for states' rights.*

Chase on March 1. Jefferson called impeachment of Justices "a farce which will not be tried again," and he was right.

For all his differences with the Republicans, John Marshall was no son of discord. Born in a log cabin near Germantown, Virginia, in 1755, he grew up near the frontier, with some tutoring for an education. He fought as an officer in the Revolution, almost freezing at Valley Forge.

After the war he practiced law, and became the leading Federalist of his state. As a young attorney and an aging Chief Justice, he was sloppily dressed and wonderfully informal out of court, fond of spending hours with friends in taverns, law offices, and drawing rooms. Even in his sixties, Marshall was still one of the best quoits players in Virginia.

When the Court met in Washington, the Justices stayed in a boardinghouse—the trip was too long, the session too short for their wives to accompany them—and Marshall's geniality brightened their off-duty hours.

Justice Joseph Story handed down a tale still told at the Court. On rainy days the Judges would enliven their conferences with wine; on other days Marshall might say, "Brother Story, step to the window and see if it doesn't look like rain." If the sun was shining, Marshall would order wine anyway, since "our jurisdiction is so vast that it must be raining somewhere."

Congress expanded that domain in 1807, creating a new circuit for Kentucky, Tennessee, and Ohio, and adding a seat to the Court. Jefferson appointed Thomas Todd, who had helped create the State of Kentucky out of his native Virginia.

LIFE IN WASHINGTON went on peacefully for months during the War of 1812. "Mrs. Madison and a train of ladies" visited the Supreme Court one day in early 1814, just as William Pinkney of Maryland, one of the country's most celebrated lawyers, was ending an argument; "he recommenced, went over the same ground, using fewer arguments, but scattering more flowers."

Rudely interrupting such diversions, the British arrived in August and burned the Capitol. Congress found shelter in the makeshift "Brick Capitol" where the Supreme Court Building stands today.

The Court, forced to shift for itself, met for a while in a house on Pennsylvania Avenue. Then it got temporary space in the Capitol. In 1819 it returned to its own semicircular room below the Senate Chamber.

"A stranger might traverse the dark avenues of the Capitol for a week," reported a visitor from New York, "without finding the

"I WAS ... FLOORED," *says Marshall with dry humor as an attendant rushes to the sprawled Chief Justice, who fell from a stepladder in a law library. The mishap reveals Marshall's relish for a joke even at his own expense. He charmed even his critics with his "great good humour and hilarity." Marshall never allowed his mental powers to corrode. He had "one ... almost supernatural faculty," wrote a lawyer, "that of developing a subject by a single glance of his mind...."*

remote corner in which Justice is administered to the American Republic. . . ."

Strangers traversing the Republic had other troubles. "I passed away my 20-dollar note of the rotten bank of Harmony, Pennsylvania, for five dollars only," a disgusted traveler complained at Vincennes, Indiana. State-chartered banks, private banks, towns, sawmills, counterfeiters—all issued notes freely. "Engravings," a Scotsman called them; no law required anyone to accept them at face value as legal tender. Everyone suffered from this chaos.

Congress had chartered the second Bank of the United States in 1816 to establish a sound national currency, to issue notes it would redeem in gold or silver. By law, the government owned a fifth of the Bank's stock and named a fifth of its directors; private investors had the rest. Unscrupulous characters got control of the Bank and mismanaged its affairs.

In the South and West, where "engravings" flourished, the Bank's branches made bad loans until the home office at Philadelphia issued new orders in August, 1818: Call in those loans, don't accept any payments but gold and silver or our own notes. Panic spread. Local banks demanded payment on their own loans, and refused to extend credit; people scrambled for money they couldn't find; land went for a song at sheriffs' auctions; shops closed; men who lost their last five dollars said bitterly, "the Bank's saved and the people are ruined."

State legislators decided to drive the Bank's branches out of their domain. Maryland passed a tax law giving the Baltimore

JUDGE ON TRIAL: *Samuel Chase (seated in foreground) hears Representative John Randolph of Virginia accuse him of "high Crimes and Misdemeanors." The House impeached Chase, an outspoken Federalist, in 1805, after he used the bench of a circuit court to denounce Jeffersonian ideals of "equal rights."*

When the Senate acquitted Chase, Republicans gave up the idea of removing Federalist judges by such proceedings. Congress has never used its constitutional powers of impeachment against any other Justice of the Supreme Court.

31

branch its choice: pay up handsomely or give up and leave. The branch ignored it. Maryland sued the cashier, James McCulloch, and won in its own courts. McCulloch took his case—that is, the Bank's—to the Supreme Court, where argument began on February 22, 1819.

Splendid in his blue coat with big brass buttons, Daniel Webster spoke for the Bank —Congress has power to charter it; Maryland has no power to tax it, for the power to tax involves a power to destroy; and never, under the Constitution, may the states tax the Union into destruction.

Luther Martin, Maryland's Attorney General, argued for his state. Where does the Constitution say Congress has power to create a national bank? he asked. Nowhere! he thundered. It lists specific 'powers, and making banks is not one of them. Mr. Webster says it *implies* such a power. Nonsense!

For the Court, Marshall defined the controversy: "a sovereign state denies the obligation, of a law . . . of the Union." An "awful" question, but "it must be decided peacefully." Because the Union is "emphatically, and truly, a government of the people," it must prevail over the states. To specific powers of Congress, the Constitution adds power to make all laws "necessary and proper" for carrying them into effect.

Marshall invoked "letter and spirit" to give that clause its meaning: "Let the end be legitimate, let it be within the scope of the constitution," and Congress may use "all means which are appropriate . . . which are not prohibited." So the Bank was constitutional; no state might tax it. Maryland's law was "unconstitutional and void."

The Court's ruling settled the conflict of law but not the political fight over the Bank's power and states' rights. Virginia's legislature made a "most solemn protest" against the decision in *McCulloch* v. *Maryland;* Ohio officials took money by force from one Bank branch. Not until President Andrew Jackson vetoed the Bank's recharter did that controversy die down.

States' rights against the powers of the Union—the issue became more explosive

WILDCAT "ENGRAVINGS" *of dubious value issued by local banks underlie a five-dollar note from the second Bank of the United States, chartered by Congress in 1816 to provide a sound currency. Caught without proper reserves during the financial panic of 1818, local banks had to foreclose on mortgages and auction land (left). People blamed banks in general, and the Bank in particular, for the severe depression that followed.*

Maryland and other states passed laws levying a heavy tax against the Bank's branches, hoping to close them. When cashier James McCulloch of the Baltimore branch ignored the law, Maryland sued him.

*The Constitution does not say Congress can charter a bank, argued the state (**McCulloch v. Maryland**). But the Supreme Court said the Bank was lawful, ruling for the first time that "implied powers" in the Constitution enable Congress to enact laws "on which the welfare of a nation essentially depends."*

33

than ever when the country faced its first great quarrel over slavery, in 1819. Southerners in Congress threatened secession and civil war; a Georgian foresaw "our houses wrapt in flames." When the House was discussing a bill to make Missouri Territory a state, a New York Representative had suggested that Congress forbid slavery there. Southerners warned, "the Union will be dissolved." The reply flashed, "let it be so!"

For months the furious debate went on. Then, in February, 1820, Senator Jesse B. Thomas of Illinois offered a compromise: Maine to be a free state, Missouri a slave state, and the rest of the Louisiana Purchase north of 36° 30' free soil forever. Henry Clay supported the plan; early in March, President James Monroe signed the laws to carry it out. Apparently the crisis was over.

In Norfolk, Virginia, P. J. and M. J. Cohen broke the law by selling six tickets in a lottery established by Congress to pay for improvements in the District of Columbia. Virginia law forbade all lotteries except its

own. A Norfolk court convicted the Cohens; they turned to the Supreme Court, pointing out that their lottery tickets were authorized by federal law.

Virginia rose in wrath; her General Assembly declared that the Court had no jurisdiction. Her lawyers fought the Cohens' request for a hearing. They warned the Supreme Court against "exciting the hostility of the state governments," which would decide how long the Union should endure. For trouble had flared again as Congress debated

FRENZIED NORTHERNERS *carry the effigy of Pennsylvania Congressman David Fullerton toward a barrel of burning tar at the county courthouse in Carlisle. The angry crowd marched through the streets in protest of Fullerton's vote for the 1820 Missouri Compromise that enabled Missouri to join the Union as a slave state. Later Fullerton resigned as a result of the feeling. Such agitation over slavery in the territories made the Dred Scott case a national issue 37 years later.*

35

BITTER PARTNERS: *Aaron Ogden (left) sued Thomas Gibbons for steamboat shipping rights in New York's harbor (below), claiming that he had exclusive rights under state law. But Gibbons maintained that an Act of Congress permitted his steamboats to enter; and the Supreme Court ruled in his favor. "In* **Gibbons v. Ogden,** *Marshall gave the classic interpretation of the Constitution's commerce clause, which made the United States a Common Market," says Justice Arthur Goldberg today.*

"DEVIL IN A SAWMILL" *cried one startled rustic as Fulton's steamboat plied the Hudson River.*

Missouri's proposed constitution and states' rights in general. Now what had been a trivial criminal case took on political importance at a time of major crisis.

Appearing for the Cohens were two of the country's most famous attorneys, David B. Ogden and William Pinkney. Ogden flatly denied the sovereignty of any state. Pinkney asserted that if any case involves federal law, federal courts must give the final decision, or the Union is "a delusion and a mockery!"

Congress adopted a new compromise on statehood for Missouri; and Marshall gave an uncompromising ruling on *Cohens* v. *Virginia*. The Court would hear the case; it existed to resolve such "clashings" of state and Union power, to keep the national government from becoming "a mere shadow." Insisting on the power of his Court, the Chief Justice boldly met the threat of secession and the claims of state sovereignty; he upheld the Union as the supreme government of the whole American people.

Then the Court heard argument on the merits of the case, and affirmed the sentence of the Norfolk court. The Cohens lost $100—their fine—and costs.

SOUTHERNERS FUMED at Marshall's stand in the Cohens' case. But in 1824, for once, a Marshall ruling met popular acclaim. Huzzas from the wharves greeted the steamboat *United States* as it chuffed triumphantly into New York harbor, her crew firing a salute, her passengers "exulting in the decision of the United States Supreme Court." That case was *Gibbons* v. *Ogden*.

Robert Fulton successfully demonstrated a steam-powered vessel on the Seine at Paris in 1803. With his

"INTEREST OF THE PUBLIC *must ...always be regarded as the main object" of charters, said Roger B. Taney. As Chief Justice he wrote this view into law in settling a controversy over two bridges at Boston. Proprietors of the Charles River toll bridge (right), under state charter, claimed Massachusetts could not let another company open a competing bridge nearby.*

In this clash of private rights and state powers, a new voice at the Supreme Court spoke for the community. In 1835, President Andrew Jackson had named Taney, his former Attorney General, to succeed Marshall as Chief Justice.

Taney lacked ornate eloquence, but his hollow, low voice and earnest delivery added clarity and persuasiveness to his statements. His defiant stand on citizens' rights during the Civil War brought him public scorn.

*In the bridge case, his first important opinion, Taney ruled that the state had power to approve construction of the much-needed Warren Bridge to serve the people. This decision (**Charles River Bridge v. Warren Bridge**) spanned a gap between established property rights and changing needs.*

CAUSEWAY OF CONTROVERSY: *Charles River Bridge in 1789 ran from the foot of Prince Street in Boston (foreground) to old*

partner, Robert R. Livingston, he held an exclusive right from New York's legislature to run steamboats on state waters, including New York harbor and the Hudson River. In 1807 their steamer splashed up the Hudson to Albany; soon money flowed into their pockets. Anyone else who wanted to run steamboats on those waters had to pay them for the privilege; some Albany men attacked the monopoly in state courts, and lost.

In 1811 the territorial legislature in New Orleans gave the partners a monopoly on the Mississippi. Now they controlled the two greatest ports in the country.

New Jersey passed a law allowing its citizens to seize steamboats owned by New Yorkers; other states enacted monopolies and countermeasures until the innocent

Charlestown, Massachusetts. The bridge,
then considered a remarkable engineering
feat, stretched 1,503 feet on 75 oak piers.

Despite predictions that strong tidal
currents or floating ice would collapse
the span, it stood more than a century.

side-wheeler was turning into a battleship.

Meanwhile three men of property went into business, then into rages, then into court. Robert Livingston's brother John bought rights in New York bay; then he sublet his waters to former Governor Aaron Ogden of New Jersey, a quarrelsome lawyer. Ogden took a partner, Thomas Gibbons, equally stubborn and hot-tempered. Soon these three were suing one another in New York courts.

Under an old Act of Congress, Gibbons had licensed two steamboats for the national coasting trade, and now he invoked this federal law to get a suit against Ogden before the Supreme Court.

Ladies crowded lawyers to hear the case. Daniel Webster spoke for Gibbons on Feb-

ruary 4, 1824; Ogden's attorneys quoted established law and precedents for two days. But Marshall avoided shoals of precedents and veering winds of state laws to set his course by the Constitution—the clause giving Congress power to regulate commerce among the states. For the first time the Court defined these words; in them Marshall found vast new currents of national strength.

More than buying and selling, he proclaimed, commerce is intercourse among nations and states; it includes navigation. For all this rich activity Congress may make rules; if its rules collide with state restrictions the latter must sink. New York's law went down before an Act of Congress.

State monopolies could not scuttle ships "propelled by the agency of fire." Steam-

boats would be as free as vessels "wafted on their voyage by the winds."

With monopolies swept away, steamboat trade spread fast and freely. Soon, by that precedent, steam cars on rails spread across state lines, across the continent.

Marshall watched, as changes came and went. "We must never forget," he had said, "that it is a *constitution* we are expounding .... a constitution, intended to endure for ages to come, and consequently, to be adapted to the various *crises* of human affairs." His actions made his words unforgettable.

When Marshall gave the Presidential oath to his cousin Thomas Jefferson in 1801, the Supreme Court was a fortress under attack. It had become a shrine when he gave the oath to Andrew Jackson in 1829.

New crises arose during Jackson's Administration. Marshall carried on his work, concerned for the country's future but not for his failing health. Jay had resigned after five years, Ellsworth after four; Marshall served from 1801 until his death in 1835. When he took the judicial oath the public hardly noticed; when he died the Nation mourned him. "There was something irresistibly winning about him," said the *Richmond Enquirer.* And *Niles' Register,* which had long denounced his decisions, said, "Next to WASHINGTON, only, did he possess the reverence and homage of the heart of the American people."

BLOODSHED IN THE SENATE: *South Carolina Representative Preston Brooks flails Senator Charles Sumner of Massachusetts after Sumner has unleashed an antislavery speech insulting Brooks's cousin, Senator Andrew Pickens Butler of South Carolina. The attack echoed a crisis in 1856: Would Kansas vote to be a free or slave state? Although the Supreme Court tried to resolve the slavery issue, passions exploded into civil war.*

"**WHIRLWIND OF MURDER,**" *wrote poet John Greenleaf Whittier of the Marais des Cygnes massacre. Near the Kansas border, proslavery riders shoot settlers who would vote for a free state in a fair election.*

About Marshall's successor, a New York journal sputtered: "The pure ermine of the Supreme Court is sullied by the appointment of that political hack, Roger B. Taney." Daniel Webster confided, "Judge Story. . . . thinks the Supreme Court is *gone,* and I think so too." The Senate debated the nomination for almost three months.

Born in Maryland in 1777, Taney attended Dickinson College, read law, and plunged into Federalist politics. While other lawyers took pride in oratory, he spoke simply in low tones that convinced juries.

Invoking freedom of speech, Taney won acquittal in 1819 for a Methodist preacher whose sermon on national sins provoked the charge of trying to stir up slave rebellion.

Suspicious of the Bank of the United

States, Taney campaigned for Andrew Jackson. In 1831 President Jackson wrote, "I have appointed mr Tauney atto. Genl." (His spelling gives the right pronunciation.) Taney supplied legal weapons in Jackson's war with the Bank, when passion ran so high that Vice President Martin Van Buren wore pistols to preside in the Senate.

Presiding over the Supreme Court for the first time, in January, 1837, Taney wore plain democratic trousers, not knee breeches, under his robe. The Court was entering a new era. A law passed in March added two new judicial circuits in the southwest and two Associate Justices. The Court be-

came unmistakably Jacksonian; conservatives dreaded what it might do to property.

But property survived. Its rights were "sacredly guarded," Taney wrote in the Charles River Bridge case, but "we must not forget that the community also have rights, and that the happiness and well being of every citizen depends on their faithful preservation." He interpreted corporation charters more strictly, state powers more generously, than Marshall had.

Meanwhile, a new agitation over human rights was growing. If it went on, wrote a Georgia planter, "we will be compelled to arm our Militia and shoot down our property

"**BID STRONG** *for this woman and child!*" *shouts a slave auctioneer on the steps of St. Louis's old courthouse. Here Dred Scott's case was first heard by state judges. It finally reached the Supreme Court. Federal marshals (right), acting under the 1850 Fugitive Slave Law, seize a Negro suspected of being a runaway slave.*

A PUBLIC MEETING
WILL BE HELD ON
THURSDAY EVENING, 2D INSTANT,
at 7⅓ o'clock, in ISRAEL CHURCH, to consider the atrocious decision of the Supreme Court in the

DRED SCOTT CASE,
and other outrages to which the colored people are subject under the Constitution of the United States.

C. L. REMOND,
ROBERT PURVIS,
and others will be speakers on the occasion. Mrs. MOTT, Mr. M'KIM and B. S. JONES of Ohio, have also accepted invitations to be present. All persons are invited to attend. Admittance free.

"**ATROCIOUS DECISION**" *cries a poster in Philadelphia, where abolitionists shouted their rage and disgust over the outcome of the Supreme Court's most famous case (**Dred Scott v. Sandford**). A slave in Missouri, Dred Scott sued for his liberty, insisting a recent sojourn on free soil in Illinois and Wisconsin Territory entitled him to be free. In 1857, the Supreme Court rejected his claim. Chief Justice Taney said no Negro could be a citizen with constitutional rights to bring suit. His opinion wounded the Court's prestige in the North, for it insisted that Congress had no power to limit expansion of slavery. Northern papers bristled with moral indignation; said one editorial, "If the people obey this decision, they disobey God."*

43

WISPY AND BENT, *Chief Justice Taney administers the Presidential oath of office to James Buchanan in 1857. In his Inaugural Address, Buchanan said the question of territorial slavery would "be speedily and finally settled" by the Supreme Court. Instead, Taney's ruling on Scott only sped the Civil War.*

"HEAP O'TROUBLE," said Scott of his decade-long lawsuit. After the Supreme Court denied Scott freedom, his owner released him from bondage. Newspaper pictures him with wife and daughters.

in the field.... tell the agitators we had rather fight them than our own negroes, and that we will do it too...."

In 1846 the United States and Mexico went to war. Unnoticed, a Negro named Dred Scott filed suit in a Missouri court. Twelve years earlier, John Emerson, an Army surgeon, had taken his slave Scott from Missouri to Illinois, where the Northwest Ordinance and state law forbade slavery. Then he had taken Scott to Fort Snelling, a frontier Army post in territory where the Missouri Compromise banned slavery forever. In 1838 he had taken Scott back to Missouri. Emerson died, and Scott sued the widow, claiming that this sojourn on free soil had made him a free man. In 1850 the Missouri court declared him free.

Mrs. Emerson appealed. The state's highest court ruled in 1852 that, free or not on free soil, Scott became a slave under state law when he went back to St. Louis.

Scott's was becoming a test case. To get it into a federal court—because federal courts have jurisdiction in suits between citizens of different states—title to Scott passed to Mrs. Emerson's brother, John F. A. Sanford of New York (misspelled "Sandford" in the records).

Claiming Missouri citizenship, Scott sued Sanford for his freedom in the federal court in St. Louis. Sanford's lawyers argued that Scott could not be a citizen because he was a slave and a Negro. The court ruled against Scott, May 15, 1854.

Congress passed the Kansas-Nebraska Act two weeks later, opening more of the West to slavery by repealing the Missouri Compromise line. Furious northerners burned its author, Stephen A. Douglas, in effigy. On July 4, abolitionist William Lloyd Garrison publicly burned a copy of the Constitution, crying, "So perish all compromises with tyranny."

Fighting broke out in Kansas and made the expansion of slavery the issue in the 1856 Presidential campaign, won by James Buchanan. The Supreme Court heard argument in *Dred Scott* v. *Sandford* in February, 1856, reached the end of its term, then heard argument again in December.

By then the whole country had heard of Dred Scott. "The Court, in trying this case, is itself on trial," said the *New York Courier*.

In February, 1857, a majority of the Justices agreed to follow precedent and say that the ruling of the highest state court was final—that Scott was a slave under state

FRANK LESLIE'S ILLUSTRATED NEWSPAPER

Entered according to Act of Congress, in the year 1857, by FRANK LESLIE, in the Clerk's Office of the District Court for the Southern District of New York. (Copyrighted June 22, 1857.)

No. 82.—VOL. IV.]   NEW YORK, SATURDAY, JUNE 27, 1857.   [PRICE 6 CENTS.

TO TOURISTS AND TRAVELLERS.

WE shall be happy to receive personal narratives, of land or sea, including adventures and incidents, from every person who pleases to correspond with our paper.

We take this opportunity of returning our thanks to our numerous artistic correspondents throughout the country, for the many sketches we are constantly receiving from them of the news of the day. We trust they will spare no pains to furnish us with drawings of events as they may occur. We would also remind them that it is necessary to send all sketches, if possible, by the earliest conveyance.

VISIT TO DRED SCOTT—HIS FAMILY—INCIDENTS OF HIS LIFE—DECISION OF THE SUPREME COURT.

WHILE standing in the Fair grounds at St. Louis, and engaged in conversation with a prominent citizen of that enterprising city, he suddenly asked us if we would not like to be introduced to Dred Scott. Upon expressing a desire to be thus honored, the gentleman called to an old negro who was standing near by, and our wish was gratified. Dred made a rude obeisance to our recognition, and seemed to enjoy the notice we expended upon him. We found him on examination to be a pure-blooded African, perhaps fifty years of age, with a shrewd, intelligent, good-natured face, of rather light frame, being not more than five feet six inches high. After some general remarks we expressed a wish to get his portrait (we had made

ELIZA AND LIZZIE, CHILDREN OF DRED SCOTT.

efforts before, through correspondents, and failed), and asked him if he would not go to Fitzgibbon's gallery and

have it taken. The gentleman present explained to Dred that it was proper he should have his likeness in the "great illustrated paper of the country," overruled his many objections, which seemed to grow out of a superstitious feeling, and he promised to be at the gallery the next day. This appointment Dred did not keep. Determined not to be foiled, we sought an interview with Mr. Crane, Dred's lawyer, who promptly gave us a letter of introduction, explaining to Dred that it was to his advantage to have his picture taken to be engraved for our paper, and also directions where we could find his domicile. We found the place with difficulty, the streets in Dred's neighborhood being more clearly defined in the plan of the city than on the mother earth; we finally reached a wooden house, however, protected by a balcony that answered the description. Approaching the door, we saw a smart, tidy-looking negress, perhaps thirty years of age, who, with two female assistants, was busy ironing. To our question, "Is this where Dred Scott lives?" we received, rather hesitatingly, the answer, "Yes." Upon our asking if he was home, she said,

"What white man arter dad nigger for?—why don't white man 'tend to his own business, and let dat nigger 'lone? Some of dese days dey'll steal dat nigger—dat are a fact."

DRED SCOTT. PHOTOGRAPHED BY FITZGIBBON, OF ST. LOUIS.   HIS WIFE, HARRIET. PHOTOGRAPHED BY FITZGIBBON, OF ST. LOUIS.

FRANK LESLIE'S ILLUSTRATED NEWSPAPER (BELOW) AND LIBRARY OF CONGRESS

AMID FLYING STONES *and bullets the first Civil War victims fall during a riot in Baltimore in 1861. Southern sympathizers attacked the 6th Massachusetts Regiment, killing four soldiers. Loyal Unionists (left) guarded the office of the city's provost marshal against the mob. The military arrested citizens suspected of disloyalty, rebellion, or treason— including John Merryman, a prominent figure in Baltimore. In Merryman's behalf, Chief Justice Taney sent Lincoln a sharp official protest denying that the President had constitutional power to suspend the protection of law, especially the writ of habeas corpus, in any emergency whatsoever.*

REGIMENTAL COLOR *of the 6th Massachusetts heralded the unit's arrival in Washington. The Baltimore rioters struck the militia April 19, 86 years to the day after Massachusetts Minutemen became the first Revolutionary War victims.*

law. Such a decision would leave to the judgment of the country two dangerously controversial issues: Whether or not a free Negro might be a citizen of the United States; and whether or not the 1820 Missouri Compromise was constitutional.

But Justices John McLean of Ohio and Benjamin R. Curtis of Massachusetts intended to dissent and say that Scott was a free man and a citizen, that Congress had constitutional power over slavery in the western territories.

In his Inaugural Address on March 4, James Buchanan promised that "in common with all good citizens" he would "cheerfully submit" to the Supreme Court's decision in Dred Scott's case.

Two days later the Justices began to deliver eight separate opinions. The majority ruled that Scott was still a slave. Three, including Taney, said no Negro, even if free, could hold citizenship in the United States.

And for the first time since 1803, the Court held an Act of Congress null and void. Under the Constitution, it announced, Congress had no power to limit the expansion of slavery by law, as the Missouri Compromise of 1820 had done.

For the first time in years, the Court came under furious attack. Almost unnoticed, Scott's owner set him free. Before the case was decided, Sanford had gone insane; before the slavery question was settled, war tried the sanity of the country.

"HAVE WE EVER had any peace on this slavery question?" asked Abraham Lincoln. The Illinois crowd yelled "No!" It

47

was 1858; Lincoln was challenging Stephen A. Douglas for a Senate seat—and challenging the Supreme Court's ruling on slavery.

Douglas defended the decision in Dred Scott's case as the pronouncement of "the highest tribunal on earth," in spite of his own objections to it. "From that decision there is no appeal this side of Heaven," he cried.

One decision settles one case, retorted Lincoln; it does not even settle the law, still less the future of the country.

Douglas won the Senate seat; in 1860 he lost the race for the Presidency; and the Republicans came to power with Lincoln.

Chief Justice Taney administered the oath of office to Lincoln, March 4, 1861, and heard him disclaim "any assault upon the Court." But Lincoln warned solemnly: "if the policy of the Government, upon vital questions affecting the whole people, is to be irrevocably fixed by decisions of the Supreme Court, the instant they are made, in ordinary litigation . . . the people will have ceased to be their own rulers. . . ."

That day the first banner of the Confederate States of America flew over the statehouse at Montgomery, Alabama.

Secession divided the Supreme Court. Justice John A. Campbell, who thought disunion wrong, resigned and went sadly home to Alabama. Justice James Moore Wayne of Georgia, last survivor of Marshall's Court, remained; until his death in 1867, he voted to sustain all the war measures the Court passed judgment on.

Justice John Catron, over 70, hurried off to uphold the laws of the United States on his secessionist circuit. Tennessee had made a military pact with the Confederacy when he got to Nashville. Dodging rebel forces, he reached St. Louis and held court there. When he returned to Nashville a citizens' committee drove him out of his home.

In Maryland, part of Taney's circuit, many favored the Union, some the South. Washington's only railroad to the north ran through Baltimore, where an angry crowd mobbed troops hurrying to defend the capital. Lincoln told the Army to suspend the writ of habeas corpus and establish martial rule, if necessary, to keep Maryland safe.

The military jailed citizens on mere suspicion; troops arrested John Merryman for taking part in the Baltimore riot and blowing up railroad bridges. Locked up in Fort McHenry, he applied for a writ of habeas corpus—a court order for proof that a prisoner is lawfully confined.

FAMOUS AUTHOR, *lawyer Richard Henry Dana, Jr., who wrote* Two Years Before the Mast, *defended Lincoln's blockade of southern coasts in the 1863 Prize Cases.*

GUNS BLAZING, *Union ships (above) chase a southern side-wheel steamer (left). A gun crew (below) prepares to fire a warning shot across the bow of another blockade runner. In 1861 Lincoln had blockaded southern ports. Owners of captured merchant ships and cargo, protesting that the Union sea barrier was unlawful, brought suit to recover their property. They said that until Congress recognized the existence of war, Lincoln had no constitutional power to order a blockade. But in the Prize Cases, the Supreme Court upheld the President's bold acts. The ruling revived the sagging morale of the Union.*

Only in "Rebellion or Invasion" when "the public safety may require it" may the privilege of habeas corpus be suspended, says the Constitution.

Hurrying to Baltimore, Chief Justice Taney issued a writ to Gen. George Cadwalader: bring Merryman to court and explain his arrest. The general sent a letter—he had to consult the President. Taney ordered a marshal to seize the general; but a sentry barred the marshal from Fort McHenry. The Chief Justice challenged the President's right to take legislative and judicial power, calling on him to uphold the law and the courts.

Lincoln did not reply; Congress upheld him. But when the emergency had passed, the government quietly brought Merryman's case to a federal court; later still, it quietly let him go free.

Resignation and death left three seats vacant at the Supreme Court. Lincoln appointed Noah H. Swayne of Ohio, Samuel F. Miller of Iowa, and his old friend from Illinois, David Davis. But no one knew what the Court would do when it heard the Prize Cases in 1863.

Before calling Congress into special session, Lincoln had authorized martial rule in Maryland, called for volunteers, pledged government credit for huge sums, and proclaimed a blockade of southern ports. To meet the crisis of war, the President swept into the realm of legislative power like an invading general. Four merchant ships, seized under Lincoln's blockade orders and condemned as prize, carried his measures before the Supreme Court.

The owners brought suit for the vessels and cargo, arguing that war alone warrants

50

"GUILTY!" *ruled this Civil War military commission that tried Lambdin P. Milligan, an Indiana lawyer, for conspiring to overthrow the government of the Union. A civilian, he demanded jury trial in a federal court.*

MILITARY COMMISSION THAT TRIED INDIANA CONSPIRATORS IN 1864.

GEN. S. COLGROVE. COL. T. LUCAS. COL. T. BENNETT   COL. B. SPOONER   COL. D. DELLART MAJOR H. BURNETT

COL. STEVENS COL. WM. MCLANE   COL. MURRAY   COL. R. WILLIAMS   COL. WA.   LIEUT. COL. HEATH

a blockade and only Congress may declare war; they denied that Lincoln's emergency powers had any reality in constitutional law.

If the Court upheld the blockade as a legal war measure, England and France might recognize the Confederacy; if it did not, the Government would have to pay huge damages for captured ships, and other war measures would be in question. Either decision would endanger the Union.

Justice Robert C. Grier spoke for himself, Wayne, and Lincoln's three appointees: The President had to meet the war as "it presented itself, without waiting for Congress to baptize it with a name"; and rebellion did not make the South a sovereign nation. Four dissenters said the conflict was the President's "personal war" until Congress recognized the insurrection on July 13, 1861. But the prairie lawyer had won his case.

Chief Justice Taney died, aged 87, in October, 1864. Lincoln's Attorney General Edward Bates wrote that his "great error" in the Dred Scott case should not forever "tarnish his otherwise well earned fame." And not long after Taney's death, victory for the Union brought vindication of his defiant stand for the rule of law.

Army authorities had arrested Lambdin P. Milligan of Indiana, a civilian, tried him before a military commission, convicted him of conspiring to overthrow the government, and sentenced him to hang. With Milligan's petition for a writ of habeas corpus, the Supreme Court considered the problem of military power over civilians.

During "the late wicked Rebellion," Lincoln had authorized such military tribunals. But, said the Justices, the federal courts in Indiana were always open to try

*In 1866, the Supreme Court (**Ex parte Milligan**) held that no military tribunal could try civilians where federal courts were "open and ready to try them" because the Constitution protects "all classes of men, at all times, and under all circumstances."*

LAMBDIN P. MILLIGAN

THE COPPERHEAD PARTY.——IN FAVOR OF *A VIGOROUS PROSECUTION OF PEACE!*

TREACHEROUS COPPERHEADS, *members of a northern political faction that sought Civil War peace at any price, threaten the Union in this 1863 cartoon from* Harper's Weekly. *A southern sympathizer, Milligan plotted with other Copperheads to raid state and U.S. arsenals for a supply of weapons, free captured Confederate soldiers from northern prison camps, arm them, and send them back to fight for the South again.*

LAST SUPREME COURT CHAMBER *in the Capitol receives a famous advocate, retired Justice Stanley Reed. "The first important case I argued for the government as Solicitor General was here in this room," he recalls. The Justice shows his grandchildren, Walter and Harriet Reed, where the Court met from 1860 to 1935.*

As do all Solicitors General, he performed the duty of deciding which lower court decisions the government would appeal to the Court, what legal stand the government would adopt, and who would argue the case for the U.S. "I was admitted to practice before the Supreme Court on April 4, 1924," says the jurist. Reed joined the Court as an Associate Justice in 1938, and he served until 1957. Below, in 1888, Chief Justice Morrison R. Waite presides over a Court session in this same room, the old Senate Chamber, sketched for Harper's Weekly.

cases like Milligan's. Therefore, under the Constitution, no military courts could try them; and, however shocking the charges, the defendants kept their rights under law.

At liberty again, Milligan sued the military for false imprisonment, and a jury awarded him damages—five dollars.

"WHAT a potato hole of a place, this!" A western lawyer, seeing the Court's first-floor room in the Capitol in 1859, thought the Justices should be "got up above ground" for some fresh air and daylight. In December, 1860, they finally moved to their new courtroom, the old Senate Chamber. With 12 rooms for their officials and records, they had more space than ever before.

Congress added a tenth seat to the Court

in 1863, and Lincoln appointed Stephen J. Field of California. To succeed Taney in 1864, he chose Salmon P. Chase of Ohio.

Ambitious and able, Chase had won fame for defending runaway slaves, served one term in the Senate and two as Governor of Ohio when Lincoln named him Secretary of the Treasury in 1861. Inexperienced in finance, Chase grappled with war costs— more than $1,000,000 a day. He planned a radical new tax on income, a new system of national banks. But plans for legal tender notes, the famous "greenbacks," upset him. War or no war, he thought, the Constitution forbade such paper money.

Lincoln sent Chase a message "not to bother himself about the Constitution. . . . I have that sacred instrument here at the

White House, and I am guarding it with great care." Reluctantly, Chase agreed.

Gossip described him addressing a mirror: "President Chase." His own hopeful publicity described his qualifications for Lincoln's place in 1864; the people declined his offer, and in June Lincoln accepted his resignation from the Treasury. Then Chase found himself named Chief Justice by the Chief Executive he had tried to supplant.

Under Radical leaders, the postwar Congress seemed determined to reconstruct the whole American government. One Representative talked of an amendment to abolish the Supreme Court; another warned President Andrew Johnson "that as Congress shall order he must obey."

Striking at Johnson, Congress lowered

the number of Associate Justices; and to protect the Reconstruction laws, it limited the Court's jurisdiction on appeals.

It was the Senate, not the Court, that tried the most dangerous case of those bitter years, the impeachment of the President.

Johnson's political enemies wanted a quick conviction. The Constitution, however, required the Chief Justice to preside; and Chase insisted on presiding as a judge, while the Senate tried legal issues as a court should. The Radicals had to let him rule on points of law; Chase gave the President's lawyers a chance to be heard. Johnson escaped conviction by one vote.

Those same bitter years saw amendments altering the Constitution. In 1865 the Thirteenth abolished slavery; in 1868 the Four-

IMPEACHED PRESIDENT *Andrew Johnson faced Radical Republicans' charges of "high Crimes and Misdemeanors" for ordering Edwin M. Stanton dismissed as Secretary of War. Chief Justice Chase (below) swears in Senator Ben Wade as impeachment court member. If Johnson had been convicted, Wade, as President pro tem of the Senate, would have succeeded him as Chief Executive.*

"FEAR NOT ... to acquit him," urged lawyer Henry Stanbery (standing, left) for President Johnson at his impeachment trial in 1868. Here Stanbery addresses Chief Justice Chase (on dais). As prosecutors, Managers for the House of Representatives sit at right. Former Associate Justice Benjamin R. Curtis (seated, center of table at left) argued that Johnson had not violated the Tenure of Office Act, which restricted removal of cabinet officers, and that the Act itself was invalid. Johnson escaped conviction by one vote. In 1926 the Supreme Court said the Act had been unconstitutional.

teenth defined United States citizenship and defended it against infringements; in 1870 the Fifteenth barred racial limits on the right to vote.

Gen. Ulysses S. Grant became President in 1869. Congress raised the number of Associate Justices back to eight, and at long last revised the circuit court system.

WHILE the South struggled with carpet-baggers and Ku Klux Klansmen, the rest of the country rushed into the splendors and scandals of the Gilded Age. Wartime greenbacks went cheap and debtors liked them; creditors wanted gold, and Chase and his Associates had to bother themselves about currency and the Constitution.

Hepburn v. *Griswold,* a private lawsuit, came before them in 1867, challenging the Legal Tender Act of 1862 and the Nation's money. Justice Wayne had died; when the remaining Judges discussed the case they divided four to four, as sharply as the rest of the country. Chase was one of those who opposed the law. If you had promised in 1861 to pay a debt in gold, he said, you could not force greenbacks on your creditor; Congress could not impair such contracts.

Then Grier, aged and sadly feeble, changed his vote so that Chase spoke for a majority. Somewhat awkwardly, the Chief Justice struck down in 1870 the law he had reluctantly defended at the Treasury.

Dissenting, Justice Miller insisted: Congress had all the powers it needed to fight a war, including power to change the currency.

Although the Court's decision applied to contracts made before February 25, 1862,

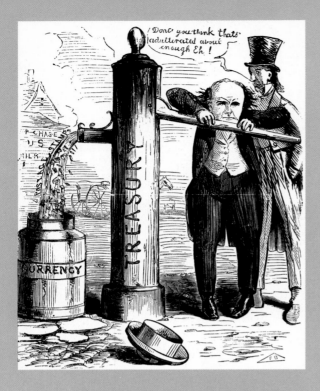

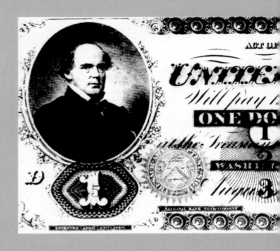

PUMPING UP THE ECONOMY, *Treasury Secretary Salmon Chase (left) tries to relieve Civil War coin shortage with postage currency, "shinplasters" worth from three to 50 cents. Note (above) carries Chase's picture. He was appointed Chief Justice by Lincoln in 1864.*

it implied that greenbacks might not be valid for later contracts. It called in question more than $350,000,000 in greenbacks. The government fretted. A Boston newspaper protested bitterly against "the country's being mangled and slaughtered, while the Supreme Court is making experiment upon the laws of currency."

Grier had resigned; Grant named William Strong and Joseph P. Bradley to the Court. They wanted to hear argument in other legal tender cases; astonished lawyers heard the Justices argue furiously on the bench about reopening the money question. After hearing the new cases in 1871, the two new Justices joined the three dissenters of *Hepburn* to overrule that decision.

Strong announced that the Legal Tender Act was constitutional; it helped pay for the war, it saved the Nation. Bradley, concurring, went further: under the monetary power, Congress could provide for paper money even in peacetime emergencies—a view the Court accepted 13 years later.

Angry editors charged that Grant had packed the Court; and even people who liked greenbacks disliked the Court's reversing itself so thoroughly and so fast.

After the spring term of 1873, Chase died. A Negro guard of honor brought his casket to the Supreme Court Chamber for a state funeral. As it rested on Lincoln's catafalque, a moment of Presidential honor came to the Chief Justice at last.

FOR CHASE'S SUCCESSOR, the Senate confirmed Grant's nomination of Morrison R. Waite in 1874. Thoroughly respectable, this 57-year-old attorney from Ohio lacked the nationwide fame of Jay or Marshall or Taney or Chase.

"I am getting the hang of the barn a little," Waite wrote modestly after a week in Washington. By 1877, when he gave the Court's decision in the Granger cases, he had gotten it thoroughly.

Corn in the woodbox fed the political prairie fire of the Granger movement. Railroads were charging so much to ship grain that farmers burned it for fuel instead of

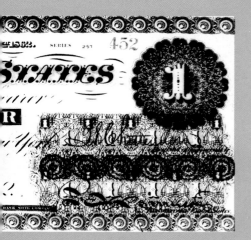

THE ONLY CHANGE *he could get, man at right laments over 1863 money problem. Meanwhile, "greenback" (above) helped pay for Union war costs; the Court eventually held such legal tender notes valid in war or peace.*

sending it for sale. Joining the Grange, or Patrons of Husbandry, farmers took their wrongs to their legislatures; four states limited freight rates by law.

Illinois farmers had unexpected allies, merchants from the Chicago Board of Trade, so disgusted at sharp practices in the grain storage business that they were willing to fight for state regulation. When Illinois law set standards for warehousing, the firm of Munn & Scott was in trouble.

With huge grain elevators in Chicago, Ira Y. Munn and George L. Scott had piled up a fortune, a name for crooked dealings, a lot of enemies, and bankruptcy.

Used to charging what the traffic would bear, the railroads found state regulation unbearable; they took their wrongs to court.

When state and federal judges upheld the "Granger laws," railroad attorneys steamed hopefully to the Supreme Court, quoting the Fourteenth Amendment on due process of law, the contract clause, and the interstate commerce clause of the Constitution. With them went lawyers for the ruined Ira Munn,

still fighting a $100 fine for illegal storage rates. If these laws stood, they argued, private property would be wrecked.

Seven Justices found all these laws valid. Like Taney, they thought community rights as sacred as corporation rights. "For us the question is one of power," said Waite; when private property affects the community, the public has constitutional power to protect its interest by law, for the common good. Firms like Munn & Scott had virtual monopolies on grain—so Illinois could exercise its power to regulate them.

Waite assigned a modest role to the courts; they must assume that a legislature knows the facts, they must accept the legislature as "the exclusive judge" of when to pass regulatory laws and what to say in them.

The railroads contended that only Congress could regulate their trade; Waite ruled that until Congress did, the states were free to act within their own borders.

The *New York Herald* said: "either the people would govern the railroads, or the railroads would govern the people. The Su-

preme Court has come to the rescue...."

But Justice Field, dissenting, called the decisions "subversive of the rights of private property." And his dissent would become the majority opinion in later decisions.

The railroads had rushed beyond state borders and laws, and Congress took action. It passed the Interstate Commerce Act in 1887, the Sherman Anti-Trust Act in 1890. Other laws—national and state—to regulate business and working conditions followed as time went by. But time proved that the legislatures were not to be the "exclusive judge." The Supreme Court began to set new limits on state power, although it did not flatly overrule the Granger decisions.

The Court also checked Congressional power. In 1895, a depression year, critics charged that the Court let property rights govern law. Waite had died, Melville W. Fuller had succeeded him as Chief Justice; of the Court that decided *Munn* v. *Illinois* in 1877, only Field survived.

When the Court decided its first antitrust case, the government lost its suit against a company controlling some 98 percent of all sugar refined in the United States. The Court conceded that the trust had a monopoly on making "a necessary of life" but denied that it had a direct effect on interstate commerce. This ruling left the Sherman Act weak, the trusts as strong as ever.

In another case, the Court seemed to ignore the needs of labor. Federal judges, under the Sherman Act, had issued a sweeping injunction against union leaders of the Pullman strike in 1894. Jailed for contempt of court, Eugene V. Debs applied to the Supreme Court for a writ of habeas corpus; the Justices denied it unanimously.

In a third case, the Court heard argument on a new federal income tax law, which took two percent of all incomes over $4,000. Famous lawyers prophesied communism, anarchy, and despotism if the law survived. With one Justice ill, the rest divided four to four on most of the law's provisions. After reargument, a five-to-four vote made the entire law unconstitutional.

Bluntly, the dissenters called this decision "the most disastrous blow ever struck at the constitutional power of Congress," "a surrender of the taxing power to the moneyed class." John Marshall Harlan (whose grandson bears his name as Associate Justice today) spoke out so sharply that the *New York Sun* called his "tone and language more appropriate to a stump address."

On the stump, William Jennings Bryan said the Court stood with the rich against the poor; other political figures took up the charge. And in 1913 the Sixteenth Amendment made the income tax constitutional after all.

UNDER THE CIVIL RIGHTS ACT of 1875, one of the last Reconstruction laws, Negro citizens brought cases before the Court, protesting their exclusion from a hotel dining room in Topeka, an opera house in New York, the dress circle of a San Francisco theater, the ladies' car on a train. In 1883, eight Justices held the act unconstitutional. The Fourteenth Amendment, they said, only gave Congress power over state action; if private citizens discriminated among one another, Congress could do nothing about it. Harlan of Kentucky, the Court's only southerner, wrote a fighting 36-page dissent.

WAREHOUSES OF GRAFT: *Chicago grain elevators of Ira Munn and George Scott loom above the Chicago River. When Munn ignored an 1871 Illinois law that curbed high storage and railway shipping rates, the state sued. The Supreme Court ruling (**Munn v. Illinois**) upheld state power to regulate businesses "affected with a public interest."*

CHAMPION OF FARMERS, *the Grange wakes the public to corrupt railroad practices. Hard hit by low grain prices, oppressed by high railroad and warehouse rates, farmers joined the Grange to protest their wrongs and fight for laws in their interest.*

CHICAGO HISTORICAL SOCIETY (LEFT) AND CULVER PICTURES, INC.

"**TREADMILL** *of uninterrupted work," said Chief Justice Morrison R. Waite, as the overworked Supreme Court of the 1880's found cases piling up faster than it could hear them. With a four-year backlog on their hands, the Justices welcomed an 1891 law creating the circuit courts of appeals to settle routine lawsuits.*

To enforce segregation by color, southern states began passing Jim Crow laws, to require equal but separate passenger cars on trains. Homer Adolph Plessy challenged the Louisiana law in 1892, and took his case to the Supreme Court. Its opinion cited many state precedents to show the "reasonableness" of such laws, and found nothing to stamp "the colored race with a badge of inferiority." Harlan dissented again.

"Our Constitution is color-blind," he wrote. "In respect of civil rights, all citizens are equal before the law." Still, the separate-but-equal doctrine of *Plessy* v. *Ferguson* controlled the law for years.

THE SPANISH-AMERICAN WAR gave the United States several heroes, including Col. Theodore Roosevelt; many islands, including Puerto Rico and the Philippines; and one baffling question: Does the Constitution follow the flag? Across the American West, it always had; pioneers took their citizenship with them, and new states joined the Union as equals.

These new islands—separate by ocean, alien by culture—seemed unfit for self-government or statehood. But the Constitution said nothing about colonies of subject peoples, unequal before the law.

In the famous "Insular Cases" the Supreme Court worked out a constitutional status for the new possessions; in effect and by necessity, the Court made law as it went along. Spectacular as the subject was, the Justices were doing the duty of every judge, applying the generalities of law to the demands of the specific case.

Cast-iron pipe and constitutional law bent in the hands of Circuit Judge William Howard Taft in 1898, as he carefully distinguished the case of the Addyston Company and other pipe manufacturers from the sugar-trust case. In the present case,

he explained, the facts were different.

These companies conspired to fix prices, said Taft, before they agreed with their customers in 36 states to deliver shipments of pipe; therefore they were within interstate commerce and the power of Congress. Price fixing restrained trade as surely as pipe contained oil, and Congress had passed the Anti-Trust Act to release trade. Free enterprise, Taft insisted, meant free competition.

When the Supreme Court affirmed Taft's ruling, other judges had a new precedent to follow and the Sherman Act a new vitality.

Energy personified, Theodore Roosevelt became President after William McKinley's assassination, and faced what he called the "absolutely vital question"—whether the United States Government had the power to control the giant corporations of the day.

Money personified, the magnificent J. P.

Morgan dominated finance, the Northern Pacific and other railroads, and the billion-dollar U. S. Steel Corporation; his ally James J. Hill had the Great Northern line. E. H. Harriman, with his Southern Pacific and Union Pacific routes and his friends in Standard Oil, had challenged Morgan and Hill for control of a railroad into Chicago.

After a fight that wrecked the stock market, the three agreed to combine forces. They organized a holding company, a New Jersey corporation called Northern Securities, and leaned back to enjoy their monopoly on transportation in the Northwest.

Roosevelt ordered the Attorney General to enforce the Sherman Act against them. In the Supreme Court their lawyers argued that only New Jersey could regulate a New Jersey corporation, that stock transactions were not within interstate commerce, that

having power did not amount to abusing it.

Justice Harlan read the Court's opinion in March, 1904, to a crowded courtroom and an anxious country. New Jersey did not have Congress at its mercy, he ruled; he called the point about stocks a mere straw man; and Congress, he said bluntly, meant to prevent the "mere existence" of such trusts. If the company was secure the Northwest was not: "the entire commerce of the immense . . . part of the United States between the Great Lakes and the Pacific at Puget Sound will be at the mercy of a single holding corporation. . . ." As the court below had ordered, the Northern Securities Company must be dissolved.

After this victory and others, the government attacked the Standard Oil empire. More than ten states had moved against it under their own antitrust laws by 1906, when federal attorneys filed suit under the Sherman Act. After 15 months of testimony that filled 21 printed volumes, federal judges in St. Louis ordered the oil trust broken up.

When the Supreme Court reviewed the case, it affirmed the order but altered the law. Congress, said Chief Justice Edward Douglass White, only meant the law to punish "unreasonable" restraint of trade. The "rule of reason" became a rule of law.

"UNREASONABLE, unnecessary and arbitrary," a violation of liberty under the Fourteenth Amendment—thus five members of the Supreme Court held a New York law unconstitutional. This law said bakers must not work more than 10 hours a day or 60 hours a week.

Joseph Lochner had a bakery in Utica, and New York fined him $20 for overworking Frank Couverette. For a second offense, he drew $50 in fines or 50 days in jail. His case reached the Court in 1905.

States, ruled Justice Rufus W. Peckham, must not pass such laws, "mere meddlesome interferences" to keep grown men from taking care of themselves. States have a "police power" to protect the public, but they may not limit such individual rights as liberty of contract: a worker must be free to make his own contract with his employer.

Justice Harlan dissented, citing evidence that bakers suffered eye and lung troubles, that New York might protect their health. And Oliver Wendell Holmes, who had joined the Court in 1902, dissented sepa-

JIM CROW LAW.

UPHELD BY THE UNITED STATES SUPREME COURT.

Statute Within the Competency of the Louisiana Legislature and Railroads—Must Furnish Separate Cars for Whites and Blacks.

Washington, May 18.—The Supreme Court today in an opinion read by Justice Brown, sustained the constitutionality of the law in Louisiana requiring the railroads of that State to provide separate cars for white and colored passengers. There was no interstate commerce feature in the case, for the railroad upon which the incident occurred giving rise to case—Plessey vs. Ferguson—East Louisiana railroad, was and is operated wholly within the State, to the laws of Congress of many of the States. The gress of many of the States. The opinion states that by the analogy of the laws of Congress, and of many of states requiring establishment of separate schools for children of two races and other similar laws, the statute in question was within competency of Louisiana Legislature, exercising the police power of the State. The judgment of the Supreme Court of State upholding law was therefore upheld.

Mr. Justice Harlan announced a very vigorous dissent saying that he saw nothing but mischief in all such laws. In his view of the case, no power in the land had right to regulate the enjoyment of civil rights upon the basis of race. It would be just as reasonable and proper, he said, for states to pass laws requiring separate cars to be furnished for Catholic and Protestants, or for descendants of those of Teutonic race and those of Latin race.

"NEXT CAR!" *a conductor directs a Negro family, motioning them to a "Colored Only" coach. Louisiana's Jim Crow Law forbade Negroes to sit with whites on trains. Attorney Albion Tourgée (above) argued for Homer Adolph Plessy, a Negro who tested the law by entering a forbidden coach. But the Supreme Court's decision in* **Plessy** v. **Ferguson** *proved the temper of the 1890's: Races could be segregated if equal facilities were provided (left). For decades after this decision, its famous "separate but equal" doctrine remained a rule of law.*

rately, to say that "a constitution is not intended to embody a particular economic theory," that laws might rest on "novel and even shocking" ideas and be constitutional.

Oregon had passed a law to keep women from working more than 10 hours a day in factories and laundries. Curt Muller, owner of a laundry in Portland, Oregon, was convicted of breaking it; he fought his conviction through state courts to the Supreme Court, relying on Peckham's opinion in *Lochner* v. *New York*. He also claimed that the Oregon statute could not meet the Constitution's demand for "due process of law."

Historically, that had meant "a fair trial." But judges were using it to protect property from laws they found unreasonable.

One reform group wanted the best possible lawyer for Oregon's case. Joseph H. Choate of New York turned it down; he didn't see why a "big husky Irishwoman should not work more than ten hours if she so desired." A famous corporation lawyer in Boston accepted—Louis D. Brandeis.

Studying Peckham's opinion in the Lochner case, Brandeis considered its reference to "common knowledge" that baking was a healthy trade. Boldly and shrewdly, he devoted only two pages of his brief to legal points; 100 cited facts from doctors, health officers, and factory inspectors to show that overworked women fell ill, turned to drink, bore sickly children and then neglected them.

No one had ever submitted such a brief to the Court. But the Justices accepted it, and praised him for it in their unani- 63

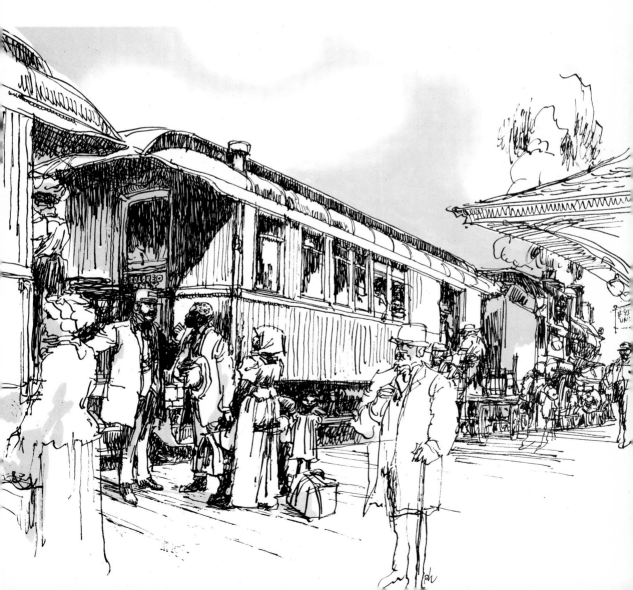

"WHY NOT LET ME IN?" asks Cuba in a 1902 cartoon. "Puerto Rico is inside." Acquiring both islands from Spain in 1898, the United States gave sovereignty to Cuba. It kept Puerto Rico; the island's canefields (below) produced quarrels among sugar growers and a lawsuit over American tariff duties on foreign goods. When the Supreme Court reviewed this case in 1901, it held that tariffs did not apply to U. S. possessions. Such suits posed the question: How does the Constitution apply to unforeseen problems— does it follow the flag? In these "Insular Cases," the Court declared that the Constitution would protect liberty anywhere under the Stars and Stripes, and would give Congress power to govern the new "American empire."

mous decision to uphold the law of Oregon.

"When an evil is a national evil, it must be cured by a national remedy," cried Senator Albert J. Beveridge of Indiana. Reformers were demanding change in politics, business, society in general; in response, Congress was assuming a "police power" for the whole country.

Disturbed by reports of filth in meat-packing plants, it passed pure food and drug laws. Shocked by stories of the "white slave trade," it passed the Mann Act. The Supreme Court upheld these laws, and others.

But when President Woodrow Wilson nominated Brandeis for Associate Justice in January, 1916, the *New York Times* thought the Court no place for "a striver after changes." William Howard Taft and Joseph H. Choate called him "not a fit per-

son" for the bench. The Senate wrangled for almost five months before confirming him.

Of all challenges to reform, child labor was the most poignant; "a subject for the combined intelligence and massed morality of American people to handle," said Senator Beveridge. In 1916 Congress passed a law to keep goods made by child labor out of interstate commerce.

As a result, John Dagenhart, less than 14, would lose his job in a textile mill in Charlotte, North Carolina. His brother, Reuben, not yet 16, would lose 12 hours of piece-work a week.

Their father asked the federal district court to enjoin the factory from obeying the law and United States Attorney William C. Hammer from enforcing it. As "a man of small means," with a large family, he com-

plained, he needed the boys' pay for their "comfortable support and maintenance." Their work was "altogether in the production of manufactured goods" and had "nothing whatsoever" to do with commerce.

When the district judge granted the injunctions, the U. S. Attorney appealed to the Supreme Court. Five Justices thought that in enacting the Child Labor Law Congress had usurped the powers of the states; such laws might destroy the federal system.

Legislation can begin where an evil begins, retorted Justice Holmes, dissenting. If Congress chooses to prohibit trade in "the product of ruined lives," the Court should not outlaw its choice. He added: "I should have thought that if we were to introduce our own moral conceptions where in my opinion they do not belong, this was

preëminently a case for upholding the exercise of all its powers by the United States."

Three Justices joined Holmes's dissent. So did Congress; it promptly set high taxes on products of child labor. But in 1922 the Court decided that this law imposed a penalty, not a tax, and held it invalid. Chief Justice William Howard Taft wrote an opinion saying the Tenth Amendment reserves problems like child labor for the states to solve.

Not until 1941 did the Court overrule its child labor decisions. Meanwhile, reformers urged an amendment to protect children, and called the Court a "Supreme Legislature." They pointed out: "The vote of one member of the Supreme Court may exceed the collective power of 435 Representatives and ninety-six Senators, or even of 100,000,000 people."

Two months after Congress declared war on Germany in April, 1917, it passed an Espionage Act that punished attempts to obstruct enlistment and discipline in the armed forces. In 1918 it passed a Sedition Act so broadly worded that almost any critical comment on the war or the government might incur a fine of $10,000, of 20 years in prison, or both.

Under the 1917 law, government attorneys filed almost 2,000 prosecutions, among them *United States* v. *"The Spirit of '76."* Only a handful of these cases reached the Supreme Court. Only after the Armistice did the Justices hear a case challenging the law by the First Amendment guarantee of free speech.

Charles T. Schenck and other members of the Socialist Party in Philadelphia were convicted of conspiring to mail circulars to drafted men. In forbidding slavery, these leaflets said, the Thirteenth Amendment forbade the draft.

For a unanimous Court, Holmes wrote that "in many places and in ordinary times" the Socialists would be within their constitutional rights. But the Bill of Rights does not protect words creating a "clear and pres-

ent danger" of "evils that Congress has a right to prevent." Schenck was sentenced to six months in jail.

But Holmes and Brandeis dissented when the 1918 Sedition Act, and leaflets in English and Yiddish, came before them. Flung from a factory window to the New York streets on August 23, 1918, these papers summoned "the workers of the world" to defend the Russian Revolution against despots. "P. S.," said some, "We hate and despise German militarism more than do your hypocritical tyrants." In the district court one defendant was acquitted; the rest went to prison.

Reviewing law and the leaflets, Holmes remarked, "Congress certainly cannot forbid all effort to change the mind of the country." He saw no national danger in the "usual tall talk" of "these poor and puny anonymities." But he saw danger in persecution of opinions, for "time has upset many fighting faiths" and the national good requires "free trade in ideas." To reach the truth, people must weigh many opinions.

"That at any rate is the theory of our Constitution. It is an experiment, as all life is an experiment," Justice Holmes concluded.

"**TRUST-BUSTER**" *Theodore Roosevelt defies the goliaths of Wall Street. James J. Hill and J. P. Morgan, through a stock monopoly called Northern Securities, controlled railroads in the northwestern states; President Roosevelt ordered a suit against them under the Sherman Anti-Trust Act. In 1904 the Supreme Court affirmed a lower court's judgment breaking up the monopoly. This decision (**Northern Securities v. U. S.**) was a victory for the public interest over the power of the trusts.*

FRENZIED SELLING *racks the stock market in the panic of 1901 when Morgan, Hill, and E. H. Harriman fought to a stalemate for control of railroad shares. Finally agreeing on a compromise, the three formed the Northern Securities Company.*

ONE OF THE GREAT DISSENTERS,
*John Marshall Harlan won fame as
a defender of democracy during 33
years as an Associate Justice, serving
from 1877 to 1911.*

*He protested sharply in the Standard
Oil case, when the Court said that no
companies may "unreasonably"
restrain trade. The Sherman Act
forbids "every" trust or combination
in restraint of interstate commerce;
Harlan thundered, "The Court has now
read into the Act of Congress words
which are not to be found there."*

*Onetime Kentucky slaveowner,
Harlan fought for the Union in the
Civil War. Appointed to the Supreme
Court by President Rutherford B.
Hayes, he carried on an ardent
battle for civil rights.*

Dissenting in **Plessy v. Ferguson,** *he
wrote: "...in view of the Constitution,
in the eye of the law, there is in this
country no superior, dominant, ruling
class of citizens.... The humblest is
the peer of the most powerful."*

*Good-humored and convivial, he
limited his disagreements to the
conference room, and enjoyed whist
parties with fellow Justices. Oliver
Wendell Holmes called him "the last
of the tobacco-spittin' judges." A
friend said that Harlan retired at night
"with one hand on the Constitution
and the other on the Bible."*

THE OCTOPUS: *Standard Oil, first of the
great American trusts, came to symbolize
wealth and power running wild, crushing*

"Any agitator who read these thirty-four
pages to a mob would not stir them to violence, except possibly against himself,"
decided one reader of Benjamin Gitlow's
"Left Wing Manifesto." But when that
pamphlet appeared in 1919, New York authorities arrested Gitlow under the state's
criminal anarchy law.

Gitlow applied to the Supreme Court.
Seven Justices upheld his conviction and
the New York statute. But they assumed—
for the first time—that freedom of speech
and of the press, which the First Amendment protects from any Act of Congress,
are among the rights which the Fourteenth

industry and government alike, as this 1904 cartoon indicates. When the Supreme Court held in 1911 that the oil monopoly must be broken up for the sake of restoring free competition, the ruling won widespread acclaim as a victory for the public.

Amendment forbids any state to abridge.

Holmes and Brandeis would have set Gitlow free. As Holmes explained, they did not think his "redundant discourse" a public danger. The majority called it "a direct incitement." Holmes replied calmly: "Every idea is an incitement."

Gitlow served three years in Sing Sing prison. Later he became one of the Communist Party's bitterest critics.

In 1925, while the Court was deciding Gitlow's case, Minnesota legislators were passing a new statute. It provided that a court order could silence, as "public nuisances," periodicals that published "malicious, scandalous, and defamatory" material.

"Unfortunately we are both former editors of a local scandal sheet, a distinction we regret," conceded J. M. Near and his partner in the first issue of the *Saturday Press,* but they promised to fight crime in Minneapolis. They called the police chief a "cuddler of criminals" who protected "rat gamblers." They abused the county attorney, who sued Near; the state's highest court ordered the paper suppressed. Citing the *Schenck* and *Gitlow* decisions, Near's lawyer appealed to the Supreme Court, which struck down the state law.

For four dissenters, Pierce Butler quoted

69

CONTROVERSIAL CONFECTIONERY: *Joseph Lochner's Home Bakery in Utica, New York, made legal history in a 1905 Supreme Court case involving working hours. His son, Joseph Lochner, Jr., stands (below) in the bakery's doorway with his mother (left) and a niece. In a damaged interior view (above), they pose with employees. Joseph Lochner, Jr., granted permission to publish these family photographs taken in 1908.*

BAKERY OWNER JOSEPH LOCHNER (*second from right*) *fought charges that he broke a New York minimum-hour statute. The Supreme Court struck down the law (***Lochner v. New York***), ruling that the Fourteenth Amendment protects "liberty of contract" between workers and employers.*

with evident distaste Near's outbursts at "snake-faced" Jewish gangsters; peace and order need legal protection from such publishers, Butler insisted.

For the majority, Chief Justice Charles Evans Hughes analyzed this "unusual, if not unique" law. If anyone published something "scandalous" a Minnesota court might close his paper permanently for damaging public morals. But charges of corruption in office always make public scandals, Hughes pointed out. Anyone defamed in print may sue for libel, he added emphatically.

However disgusting Near's words, said Hughes, the words of the Constitution controlled the decision, and they demand a free press without censorship. Criticism may offend public officials, it may even remove them from office; but trashy or trenchant, it is liberty unabated at the Supreme Court.

How men use liberty has confronted the Justices again and again, in cases of violence as well as scandal.

Frank Moore faced an Arkansas electric chair; so did Ed Hicks, J. E. Knox, Ed Coleman, and Paul Hall, all Negroes. When a federal district court said that it could not help them, they took their petition for a writ of habeas corpus to the Supreme Court, and raised the question: How does the Constitution protect the right to a fair trial in state courts?

Announcing the ruling of the Court, Justice Holmes gave their story as it appeared from the trial record and the sworn statements of other witnesses:

Negro sharecroppers in the cotton country around Elaine, Arkansas, decided that their landlords oppressed and cheated them. On the night of September 30, 1919, they

PHILOSOPHIC DISSENTER, *Oliver Wendell Holmes, a dashing figure who spoke with the eloquence of a romantic, created new concepts in judicial thinking. As a Justice he inspired generations of lawyers to shun classic attitudes of jurisprudence and recognize that law changes with society's needs. Highly sophisticated, Holmes approached law with a skeptical and objective mind.*

Chosen for the Court by President Theodore Roosevelt in 1902, Holmes boldly accused his Associates of reading into the Constitution economic rather than legal theories. When the Court killed a state law that set minimum hours for bakers (Lochner v. New York), he wrote one of the most famous dissents in history: "... a constitution is not intended to embody a particular economic theory.... It is made for people of fundamentally differing views...."

Holmes's life spanned almost 94 years. Wounded three times in the Civil War, he lived to serve the law until 1935. Appointed a Justice at 61, he worked in a world of ideas and values, and took pleasure "just in trying to exhibit some hint of horizons." Master of his profession, he retired from the Court at age 90.

met in the Hoop Spur church to plan ways of getting help from a lawyer. Armed white men attacked them; in the fight that followed, one white man was killed.

News and rumors spread; armed posses hurried to Elaine. Negroes were hunted down and shot, even women working cotton in the fields. On October 1, Clinton Lee, a white man, was killed; Moore, Hicks, Knox, Coleman, and Hall were arrested for murder.

The Governor asked the Army to restore order, and named a Committee of Seven to investigate the riots. When a lynch mob surrounded the jail, soldiers stood guard while the committee promised that the law would execute the five murderers. The mob waited to see what would happen.

Two white men and several Negroes swore later that the committee tortured Negroes until they agreed to testify against the prisoners. Indicted by a white grand jury for first-degree murder, the defendants faced a white trial jury on November 3; a threatening crowd filled the courthouse and the streets outside. In 45 minutes the trial was over; in two or three minutes the jury gave its verdict: "Guilty."

From the affidavits presented to the Court, Holmes concluded, "if any prisoner by any chance had been acquitted by a jury he could not have escaped the mob."

All appeals in the state courts had failed.

Normally, federal courts will not interfere with the courts of any state on matters of state law. But, warned Holmes, if "the whole proceeding is a mask"—if "an irresistible wave of public passion" sweeps the prisoners through the courts "to the fatal end"—then nothing can prevent the Supreme Court "from securing to the petitioners their constitutional rights."

The district judge should have examined the facts for himself, Holmes ruled, to see if the story in Moore's petition was true and if the state had not given its prisoners a fair trial. *Moore* v. *Dempsey* went back for the district judge to hear.

Eventually, all five defendants went free; so did nearly 100 other Negroes arrested during the riots. Federal judges had a new precedent, citizens a new safeguard. Justice may wear a blindfold, ruled the Supreme Court, but not a mask.

Alabama militia had machine guns on the courthouse roof, said newspaper reports from Scottsboro; mobs had a band playing "There'll Be a Hot Time in the Old Town Tonight," and those boys in jail had no chance for a fair trial—just because of a trip aboard a freight train.

Victoria Price and Ruby Bates, two white mill workers, were riding a slow freight from Chattanooga on their way home to Huntsville on March 25, 1931. Across the Alabama line, white and Negro hoboes on board got into a fight; some jumped and some were thrown from the train. Alerted by telephone, a sheriff's posse stopped the train, arrested the nine Negroes still on it, and took them to jail in the Jackson County seat, Scottsboro. Then Victoria Price claimed they had raped her and Ruby Bates.

Doctors found no proof of this story, but a frenzied crowd gathered swiftly. Ten thousand people, many armed, were there a week later when the nine went on trial.

OVERWORKED LAUNDRESS *in the shop of Curt Muller (above, arms folded) led to a Court ruling: states may enforce minimum hours for women (**Muller** v. **Oregon**). Lawyer Louis D. Brandeis (below) revolutionized legal briefs by using medical and sociological facts to show evils of unregulated working conditions.*

"THE NEW HAND." *Young, wide-eyed girl reports for her first day at a textile mill in this cartoon—one of many attacks on the "national evil" of child labor in the early 1900's. Workers often developed tuberculosis in the warm, moist air of poorly ventilated spinning rooms such as the one shown below.*

Because state law provided a death penalty, it required the court to appoint one or two defense lawyers. At the arraignment, the judge told all seven members of the county bar to serve. Six made excuses.

In three trials, completed in three days, jurors found eight defendants guilty; they could not agree on Roy Wright, one of the youngest. The eight were sentenced to death.

Of these nine, the oldest might have reached 21; one was crippled, one nearly blind; each signed his name by "X"—"his mark." All swore they were innocent.

On appeal, Alabama's highest court ordered a new hearing for little Eugene Williams; but it upheld the other proceedings.

When a petition in the name of Ozie Powell reached the Supreme Court, seven Justices agreed that no lawyer had helped the defendants at the trials. Justice George Sutherland wrote the Court's opinion. Facing a possible death sentence, unable to hire a lawyer, too young or ignorant or dull to defend himself—such a defendant has a constitutional right to counsel, and his counsel must fight for him, Sutherland said.

Sent back for retrial, the cases went on. *Norris* v. *Alabama* reached the Supreme Court in 1935; Chief Justice Hughes ruled that because qualified Negroes did not serve on jury duty in those counties, the trials had been unconstitutional.

"We still have the right to secede!" retorted one southern official. Again the prisoners stood trial. Finally Alabama dropped rape charges against some; others were paroled; one escaped.

The Supreme Court's rulings stood —if a defendant lacks a lawyer and a fairly chosen jury, the Constitution can help him.

And the Constitution forbids any state's prosecuting attorneys to use evidence they know is false; the Court announced this in 1935, when

BROWN BROTHERS (ABOVE) AND LEWIS HINE COLLECTION, LIBRARY OF CONGRESS

CHOKING DUST *congests the lungs of boys picking slate from coal in a Pennsylvania mine. Below, a Louisiana cannery breaks state law by employing children to shuck oysters. For their work, youngsters usually got only a few cents a day. In 1918 and 1922 the Supreme Court held invalid federal laws against child labor; it overruled these decisions in 1941.*

75

FILM EPIC *or espionage? The case of* The Spirit of '76 *arose like almost 2,000 others when the 1917 Espionage Act endangered freedom of speech during the feverish days of World War I. Poster at right announces the premiere of '76 in Los Angeles. The 12-reel photoplay portrayed events of the American Revolution— clashes between patriots and English and signing of the Declaration of Independence.*

Federal prosecutors charged that the film's producer, Robert Goldstein, a suspected German sympathizer, tried to arouse hatred between America and her World War I ally, England, by inserting scenes showing British soldiers committing atrocities in the Revolutionary War. Officials seized the film and Goldstein was convicted (United States v. "The Spirit of '76").

Under a new law, the 1918 Sedition Act, similar cases in the lower courts further threatened freedom of speech. Only after the Armistice did the Supreme Court review a scant number of these cases; Goldstein's was not among them. His movie script survives in the Library of Congress. But the film is lost. Weeks of intensive search uncovered these rare photographs made during the filming and owned by Charles E. Toberman, a Los Angeles resident, who invested money in the 1917 extravaganza.

COURTESY CHARLES E. TOBERMAN

Tom Mooney had spent nearly 20 years behind the bars of a California prison.

To rally support for a stronger Army and Navy, San Franciscans organized a huge parade for "Preparedness Day," July 22, 1916. As the marchers set out, a bomb exploded; 10 victims died, 40 were injured. Mooney, known as a friend of anarchists and a labor radical, was convicted of first-degree murder; soon it appeared that the chief witness against him had lied under oath. President Wilson persuaded the Governor of California to commute the death sentence to life imprisonment. For years labor called Mooney a martyr to injustice.

Finally Mooney's lawyers applied to the Supreme Court for a writ of habeas corpus, and won a new ruling—if a state uses perjured witnesses, knowing that they lie, it violates the Fourteenth Amendment's guarantee of due process of law; it must provide ways to set aside such tainted convictions. The case went back to the state. In 1939 Governor Culbert Olson granted Mooney a pardon; free, he was almost forgotten.

"JUSTICE DELAYED is justice denied" —the Supreme Court saw this in 1887, when it was almost four years behind in its work. Appealing to the public, Chief Justice Waite sought "relief for the people against the tedious and oppressive delays" of federal justice. In 1891 Congress passed a law that gave each circuit a court of appeals with power to make a final decision in a great many cases. This law also ended the Justices' trips on circuit duty. Before long the Supreme Court was keeping up with its schedules. But as new laws regulated business and working conditions, and suits challenging these laws reached the courts, overloaded dockets plagued the Justices again.

After Fuller's death in July, 1910, President Taft broke tradition by naming an Associate Justice, Edward Douglass White, for Chief.

When White died in 1921, President Harding made Taft Chief Justice, the only former Chief Executive ever to hold the highest judicial office. Taft was vastly delighted, for the Chief Justiceship, not the Presidency, had always been the honor he wanted most.

Considering the clogged machinery of the federal courts, where the case load was rising again, Taft remarked: "A rich man can stand the delay . . . but the poor man always suffers." The new Chief Justice set out to improve the whole federal judiciary.

He planned the Conference of Senior Circuit Court Judges, a source of many reforms in judicial practice. The law establishing the conference permitted judges of one area to help elsewhere on courts swamped with work. Then Taft broke tradition to lobby for the "Judges' Bill," passed in 1925.

By limiting the right of appeal, this law let the Supreme Court devote its attention to constitutional issues and important questions of federal law. In most cases since 1925, the parties ask permission to be heard; the Justices grant or deny it at discretion.

Before gaining freedom to choose cases, the Court astonished the country in 1923 by a choice of precedents to decide *Adkins* v. *Children's Hospital*. In the majority opinion, Justice Sutherland returned to the "meddlesome interferences" doctrine of *Lochner* v. *New York,* the bakery case of 1905.

Congress had passed a law to guarantee minimum wages for women and children

EUGENE V. DEBS (*speaking above*) *fought for workers' rights. For his role in the 1894 Pullman strike, he went to jail. Labor bitterly attacked the Supreme Court for letting his sentence stand.*

BEHIND BARS *on a sedition charge, Socialist Debs wins Presidential nomination in 1920. He lost to Warren Harding, who set him free.*

working in the District of Columbia. A children's hospital attacked the law; the case reached the Supreme Court. Five Justices agreed that the law violated the due process clause of the Fifth Amendment and the right to liberty of contract. Sutherland hinted that since women had won the right to vote they were legally equal to men, so Congress should not single them out for special protection.

"It will need more than the Nineteenth Amendment to convince me that there are no differences between men and women," Holmes retorted, dissenting, "or that legislation cannot take those differences into account." On the "dogma" of liberty of contract, he remarked: "pretty much all law consists in forbidding men to do some things that they want to do, and contract is no more exempt from law than other acts."

Taft also dissented. He had always supposed, he said, that *Lochner* had been overruled by later decisions; and, he added, poor workers cannot meet an employer on an equal level of choice.

But Arizona, Arkansas, and New York saw their minimum-wage laws go down under the *Adkins* precedent.

Justice Sutherland always believed that judges were the best guardians of liberty. Chosen for learning, ability, and impartiality, judges were safer guides than any other men. Courts were wiser than crowds.

"I am an optimist in all things," Sutherland said once. He felt sure that evolution's universal laws were making the world better, that meddlesome legislation could only bring trouble. Often he spoke for the famous "four horsemen"—himself, Pierce Butler, James C. McReynolds, and Willis Van Devanter. With them and one other Justice, Sutherland could say what laws were valid.

By 1930 Harvard Professor Felix Frankfurter took stock: "Since 1920 the Court has invalidated more legislation than in fifty years preceding." When Taft retired that year, President Hoover wanted Charles Evans Hughes for Chief Justice. Debating the appointment, one Senator accused the Justices of "fixing policies for the people . . . when they should leave that to Congress," another called the Court "the economic dictator in the United States." But the Senate

COMMUNIST CANDIDATES, *William Z. Foster (left) and his running mate Benjamin Gitlow lost miserably in the 1928 Presidential race. In 1925 the Supreme Court had upheld a New York conviction of Gitlow for publishing the "Left Wing Manifesto." This ponderous article, calling workers to rise against capitalism, appeared in* The Revolutionary Age *(above).*

confirmed Hughes for Chief, and Owen J. Roberts for Associate a few months later.

Nicknamed the "roving Justices," Hughes and Roberts sometimes joined the "four horsemen," sometimes joined three Judges more willing to accept laws however meddlesome. These three were Brandeis, Harlan Fiske Stone, and Holmes until he retired in 1932. Benjamin N. Cardozo succeeded him, and often voted with Brandeis and Stone.

WHEN THE STOCK MARKET collapsed in 1929 and the American economy headed toward ruin, President Hoover called for emergency measures. The states tried to cope with the general disaster. Before long, cases on their new laws began to reach the Supreme Court. Franklin D. Roosevelt won the 1932 Presidential election, and by June, 1933, Congress had passed 15 major laws for national remedies.

Almost 20,000,000 people depended on federal relief by 1934, when the Supreme Court decided the case of Leo Nebbia. New York's milk-control board had fixed the lawful price of milk at nine cents a quart; the state had convicted Nebbia, a Rochester grocer, of selling two quarts and a five-cent loaf of bread for only 18 cents. Nebbia had appealed. Justice Roberts wrote the majority opinion, upholding the New York law; he went beyond the 1887 decision in the Granger cases to declare that a state may regulate any business whatever when the public good requires it. The "four horsemen" dissented; but Roosevelt's New Dealers began to hope their economic program might win the Supreme Court's approval after all.

They were wrong. Considering a New Deal law for the first time, in January, 1935, the Court held that one part of the National Industrial Recovery Act gave the President too much lawmaking power.

The Court did sustain the policy of reducing the dollar's value in gold. But a five-to-four decision in May made a railroad pen-

U. S. ARMY TROOPS *guard Negroes rounded up near Elaine, Arkansas, after racial violence broke out in the autumn of 1919. Negro sharecroppers had felt white landlords were cheating them. Local authorities feared subsequent riots were the beginning of a mass-murder plot.*

sion law unconstitutional. Then all nine Justices ruled out a law to relieve farm debtors, and the whole NRA; and Roosevelt denounced their "horse-and-buggy" definition of interstate commerce.

While the Court moved into its splendid new building, criticism of its decisions grew sharper and angrier. The whole federal judiciary came under attack as district courts issued—over a two-year period—some 1,600 injunctions to keep Acts of Congress from being enforced. But the Court seemed to ignore the clamor.

Farming lay outside Congressional power, said six Justices in 1936; they called the Agricultural Adjustment Act invalid for dealing with state problems. Brandeis and Cardozo joined Stone in a scathing dissent: "Courts are not the only agency . . . that must be assumed to have capacity to govern." But two decisions that followed denied power to both the federal and the state governments.

In a law to strengthen the chaotic soft-coal industry and help the almost starving miners, Congress had

SCENE OF VIOLENCE: *Negro sharecroppers air grievances in Hoop Spur church near Elaine. White men park nearby. Suddenly gunfire explodes into the "Elaine Massacre." Frank Moore and other Negroes were sentenced to die for murder. The Supreme Court considered their claim that mob domination barred fair trial, and returned the case to a federal court for investigation (**Moore v. Dempsey**). Eventually, all defendants went free.*

81

dealt with prices in one section, with working conditions and wages in another. If the courts held one section invalid, the other might survive. When a test case came up, seven coal-mining states urged the Court to uphold the Act, but five Justices called the whole law unconstitutional for trying to cure "local evils"—state problems.

Then they threw out a New York law that set minimum wages for women and children; they said states could not regulate matters of individual liberty.

By forbidding Congress and the states to act, Stone confided bitterly to his sister, the Court had apparently "tied Uncle Sam up in a hard knot."

That November Roosevelt won reelection by a margin of ten million votes; Democrats won more than three-fourths of the seats in Congress. The people had spoken. Yet the laws their representatives passed might stand or fall by five or six votes in the Supreme Court. Roosevelt, aware that Congress had changed the number of Justices six times since 1789, sent a plan for court reform to the Senate on February 5, 1937. Emphasizing the limited vision of "older men," Roosevelt asked Congress for power to name an additional Justice when one aged 70 did not resign, until the Court should have 15 members. (Six were already over 70; Brandeis was 80.) Roosevelt said the Court needed help to keep up with its work.

Even staunch New Dealers boggled at this plan; it incurred criticism as sharp as any the Court had ever provoked. Chief Justice Hughes calmly pointed out that the Court was keeping up with its work. And in angry editorials and thousands of letters to Congress the public protested the very idea of "packing" the Court.

Before the President revealed his plan, five Justices had already voted to sustain a state minimum-wage law in a case from Washington; on March 29, the Court announced that the law was constitutional.

On April 12, Chief Justice Hughes read the majority opinion in *National Labor Relations Board* v. *Jones & Laughlin Steel Corporation*. It upheld the Wagner Act, the first federal law to regulate disputes between capital and labor. Hughes gave interstate commerce a definition broader than the Jones & Laughlin domain—mines in Minnesota, quarries in West Virginia, steamships on the Great Lakes. Although the case

82

turned on a union dispute at one plant in Pennsylvania, he said, a company-wide dispute would paralyze interstate commerce. Congress could prevent such evils and protect union rights.

Under these two rulings, Congress and the states were free to exercise powers the Court had denied just a year before. Stubbornly the "four horsemen" dissented. But Van Devanter announced that he would retire. By autumn the fight over the Court was a thing of the past.

As Lincoln said in 1861, the people would rule themselves; they would decide vital questions of national policy. But, as firmly as Lincoln himself, they disclaimed "any assault upon the Court." In one of the Supreme Court's greatest crises, the people chose to sustain its power and dignity.

DECISIONS CHANGED dramatically in the "constitutional revolution" of 1937. So did the Court when President Roosevelt made appointments at last.

In 1937 he named Senator Hugo L. Black; Solicitor General Stanley Reed in 1938; Felix Frankfurter and William O. Douglas, Chairman of the Securities and Exchange Commission, in 1939. Attorney General Frank Murphy came to the bench in 1940; Senator James F. Byrnes of South Carolina, in 1941.

When Hughes retired that year, Roosevelt made Stone Chief Justice and gave his seat as Associate to Attorney General Robert H. Jackson. How the "new Court" would meet old problems soon became clear.

Congress passed the Fair Labor Standards Act in 1938. It banned child labor, regulated hours, and set minimum wages—25 cents an hour—in interstate commerce. *United States* v. *Darby Lumber Co.* brought the law before the Court in 1941.

If the Justices followed the child labor decisions of 1918 and 1922, they would veto the law; but all nine called it valid.

But new problems tested the Court as it was defining civil liberties. Danger from abroad made the case for patriotism and freedom in America more urgent; in the "blood purge" of 1934, Adolf Hitler had announced, "I became the supreme judge of the German people."

Under God's law, the Commandments in the Book of Exodus, members of Jehovah's Witnesses refuse to salute a flag.

JUDICIAL ARCHITECT, *William Howard Taft, tenth Chief Justice, streamlined the Nation's system of legal review. At his persuasion, Congress passed the "Judges' Bill" in 1925. This stripped the Supreme Court of routine cases, leaving Justices free to hear only suits that involved major constitutional questions and problems of federal law.*

He won another victory when Congress provided funds for the first Supreme Court Building. With the Justices in 1929 (left), Taft studies architect Cass Gilbert's model. When the cornerstone was laid in 1932, Chief Justice Charles Evans Hughes said of Taft, who had died two years before: "This building is the result of his intelligent persistence."

Taft realized a lifelong ambition when President Harding appointed him Chief Justice in 1921. Taft later wrote, "...the court...next to my wife and children, is the nearest thing to my heart in life." Before becoming Chief Justice, he served as the twenty-seventh President—the only man to hold both offices.

BEWILDERED NEGRO YOUTHS *walk under guard of state militia toward the Jackson County courthouse at Scottsboro, Alabama. Charged with assaulting two white women, the defendants stood their first trial in 1931 when 19-year-old Ruby Bates (left, on witness stand) said the Negroes had attacked her and a friend. At a later trial in 1933 she swore that her original story was a lie, but her repentant testimony failed to convince the jury. She later led a demonstration to the White House in an appeal for the freedom of the nine Negroes.*

When Lillian and William Gobitas (misspelled "Gobitis" in the record), aged 12 and 10 in 1935, refused to join classmates in saluting the Stars and Stripes, the Board of Education in Minersville, Pennsylvania, decided to expel them for "insubordination." With help from other Witnesses and the American Civil Liberties Union, their father sought relief in the federal courts. The district court and the circuit court of appeals granted it. In 1940 the school board turned to the Supreme Court.

Considering the right of local authorities to settle local problems, eight Justices voted to uphold the school board's "secular regulation." Justice Frankfurter wrote the majority opinion. He told Justice Stone that his private idea "of liberty and toleration and good sense" favored the Gobitas family, but he believed that judges should defer to the actions of the people's elected representatives.

Hitler's armies had stabbed into France when Frankfurter announced the Court's ruling on June 3, 1940; Stone read his dissent with obvious emotion, insisting that the Constitution must preserve "freedom of mind and spirit."

Law reviews criticized the Court for setting aside the issue of religious freedom. Witnesses suffered violent attacks around the country; many states expelled children from school for not saluting the flag.

SCOTTSBORO BOYS *confer with lawyer Sam Leibowitz, who later became a famous New York judge. His masterly defense focused world attention on Alabama trials where eight of the defendants were convicted and sentenced to death in the electric chair. The spotlight of the Scottsboro cases fell on Haywood Patterson (seated). When Leibowitz and his co-counsel showed that qualified Negroes had been barred from jury duty, and claimed that the boys had been denied a fair trial, the Supreme Court reversed their convictions. Alabama tried them again. In an Alabama courtroom with Leibowitz (opposite), Patterson holds a horseshoe for good luck. It failed him. He was four times tried and convicted of attacking two white girls. In 1948 he escaped prison and was never recaptured.*

West Virginia law required all schools to teach "Americanism," and in 1942 the State Board of Education ordered all teachers and pupils to salute the flag. A child who refused might be punished as a "delinquent," his parents might be fined or jailed.

Walter Barnette and other Witnesses with school-age children sued for a federal injunction against these penalties; in 1943 the Supreme Court heard the case argued.

On Flag Day, June 14, the Court flatly overruled and repudiated the *Gobitis* decision. For the majority, Justice Jackson rejected the idea that a child's forced salute would foster national unity. He singled out as a "fixed star in our constitutional constellation" this fact—"no official, high or petty," can prescribe orthodoxy in politics, nationalism, or religion, for any citizen.

Justice Frankfurter still upheld the state's action against his own "purely personal" view, saying: "One who belongs to the most vilified and persecuted minority in history is not likely to be insensible to the freedoms guaranteed by our Constitution."

AGITATOR AND MARTYR *for labor, Tom Mooney, leaves San Quentin in 1939. Charged with murder for deaths in a 1916 Preparedness Day bombing, he escaped the gallows when facts indicated he had been convicted on perjured testimony. In 1918 the Governor of California commuted his sentence to life in prison; 20 years later, he was pardoned.*

"In this solemn hour we pledge our fullest cooperation to you, Mr. President, and to our country," said a telegram to President Roosevelt, December 7, 1941, from the Japanese American Citizens League, at news of the Japanese attack on Pearl Harbor.

By the spring of 1942 such citizens were a vilified minority in their own country. In February the President signed Executive Order 9066, authorizing the War Department to remove "any and all persons" from military areas it might name; Congress approved in a law passed March 21. The Western Defense Command ordered everyone of Japanese ancestry to stay indoors from 8 p.m. to 6 a.m. In May the Army ordered such persons to report for evacuation to "relocation centers"—detention camps.

Gordon K. Hirabayashi, a senior at the University of Washington, thought it was his duty as a citizen to disobey both these orders, to defend his constitutional rights. Convicted and sentenced to three months in prison, he applied to the Supreme Court.

Chief Justice Stone spoke for all nine in June, 1943: the curfew was within the war power of the President and Congress. Concurring, Douglas wrote that the Court did not consider the wisdom of the order; Murphy insisted that the government could take such measures only in "great emergency."

In *Korematsu* v. *United States,* argued in October and decided on December 18, 1944, the Court upheld an Army order banishing civilians of Japanese ancestry from the west coast—adults, foster children in white homes, citizens "with as little as one-sixteenth Japanese blood." Justice Black wrote the majority opinion, mentioning Toyosaburo Korematsu's unquestioned loyalty. Orders affecting one racial group are "immediately suspect," said Black, but the Court would accept the order "as of the time it was made," under the war power.

Three Justices dissented, calling the order "a clear violation of Constitutional rights," "utterly revolting among a free people."

That same day, the Court unanimously ordered the Central Utah Relocation Center to release Miss Mitsuye Endo. The War Relocation Authority had conceded she was a loyal, law-abiding citizen, but it had not allowed her to leave the center freely.

WIDE WORLD

VICTIMS OF TERRORIST BOMBING: *During Preparedness Day parade in San Francisco, spectators and marchers fell when a bomb exploded just off Market Street (above). Mooney claimed he was man on parapet (right), more than a mile from the disaster. Convicted nevertheless, he applied to the Supreme Court (**Mooney v. Holohan**). It ruled that the Constitution forbids use in state courts of testimony known to be perjury.*

Justice Douglas's opinion warned that power to defend the community is not power to detain trustworthy citizens. Federal courts may issue writs of habeas corpus in such cases, he said. "Loyalty is a matter of the heart and mind," added Douglas, "not of race, creed, or color."

AS DEFENSE COUNSEL for Richard Quirin and seven other prisoners, Col. Kenneth C. Royall and Col. Cassius M. Dowell decided that to obey one order of their Commander in Chief they had to defy another. Their clients, all German-born, had lived in America but returned before Pearl Harbor to study sabotage techniques at a school near Berlin.

In dense midnight fog on June 12, 1942, a German submarine edged toward Amagansett Beach, Long Island, to land Quirin and three comrades, in German uniform, in a rubber boat. On the beach they met an unarmed Coast Guardsman who pretended to believe their story about fishing, then went off to get help. Armed, his patrol hurried back—to hear U-boat diesels offshore, to dig up cases of TNT and bombs disguised

as pen-and-pencil sets, to notify the police and the Federal Bureau of Investigation.

Five nights later, Herbert Haupt, Werner Thiel, Edward Kerling, and Hermann Neubauer landed safely at Ponte Vedra Beach, Florida, from another U-boat. None of the saboteurs damaged his target. On June 27, the FBI announced the arrest of all eight.

President Roosevelt appointed a military commission to try them as spies under the Articles of War, and Colonels Royall and Dowell to defend them. He issued a proclamation closing all civilian courts to such enemies, but the defense decided, in duty to their clients, to disobey this. Challenging the commission's legal authority, they sought writs of habeas corpus from the Court.

After two days of hearing and questioning lawyers for both sides, the Court said that Congress, in the Articles of War, had provided for commissions to try such cases; that the President had lawfully appointed one; that the writs would not issue.

The President announced on August 8 that all the saboteurs had been convicted, six executed. Two who had cooperated with the FBI went to prison at hard labor.

STILL SMILING *31 years later, Leo Nebbia, former Rochester, New York, grocer (left), holds two bottles of milk, which has more than tripled in cost since he sold it for nine cents a quart during the Great Depression. Nebbia appealed to the Supreme Court after being convicted of breaking a state minimum-price law passed to protect the New York milk industry in the face of damaging price wars.*

The grocer maintained that the state could not control the prices of goods and commodities he sold. But in 1934 the Supreme Court sustained the state law by ruling in **Nebbia v. New York** *that prices may be regulated when public need requires such measures. Nebbia paid a five-dollar fine. Picture at right appeared in a newspaper that reported the outcome of Nebbia's case.*

Today, his son, Vincent, owns the store, still operating in the same location but four times larger. Nebbia, now a Las Vegas, Nevada, realtor, made a special journey to Rochester for the present-day picture.

In its published opinion the Supreme Court discussed precedents from 1780 to recent years. And it set another precedent —no proclamation from the White House would close the doors of the Court. An executive order would not annul its power to review government actions under law.

Bridges and aluminum plants survived the saboteurs' visit unharmed; a friend and a father did not. From Werner Thiel's days in New York, watched by the FBI, came *Cramer* v. *United States*. For the first time the Supreme Court reviewed a conviction for treason; a five-to-four vote decided that the conviction could not stand.

Justice Jackson, for the majority, explained why. The Constitution outlines the law of a most intricate crime in two sentences "packed with controversy and difficulty," he said. Treason against the United States lies "only in levying War against them, or in adhering to their Enemies, giving them Aid and Comfort." Unless a person confesses "in open Court" or two witnesses testify "to the same overt Act" of treason, he cannot be found guilty.

The jury that convicted Anthony Cramer, a naturalized citizen, heard how he met Thiel and Kerling, "enemies of the United States," at an inn and a cafeteria. Two witnesses swore that they drank and talked "long and earnestly." But no one proved what they said.

The jury had no evidence that Cramer gave the enemies shelter or advice "or even paid for their drinks." Before the war, Thiel and Cramer had shared "a small and luckless delicatessen enterprise." If they met in public "to tipple and trifle" this did not prove Cramer's treason in law.

Acts innocent by nature may serve a treasonous plan, Justice Douglas insisted for the four dissenters.

Another jury considered this point when Hans Max Haupt, a naturalized citizen, stood trial for treason. His son Herbert, one of the saboteurs, had already been executed. Witnesses swore that he had sheltered his son for six days in his Chicago apartment; he had helped him buy a car; he had helped him try to get back a job at a plant making lenses for the secret Norden bombsight. All these actions were harmless, even if proved, Haupt's lawyers argued.

UNFURLED "BLUE EAGLE," *symbol of the National Recovery Administration (NRA), rises above a delegation (left) headed by New York City's Mayor Fiorello H. La Guardia, in center foreground. President Franklin D. Roosevelt set up the NRA in 1933 under one of the most sweeping laws ever passed by Congress to regulate commerce among the states.*

As an emergency measure, the NRA attempted, through federal control, to promote the recovery of the Nation's industry, create work for the mass of Great Depression jobless, and provide purchasing power to drain the surplus of food and manufactured goods piled up in warehouses throughout the country.

"What hit me?" wonders the New Deal (right), caught by a whirlwind decision of the Supreme Court.

VICTORIOUS BROTHERS, *Aaron (left) and Alex Schechter, shoulder lawyer Joseph Heller who won their celebrated lawsuit— the "Sick Chicken Case," a deathblow to the NRA. The government had indicted the brothers, poultry dealers in Brooklyn, New York, for breaking the NRA's "Live Poultry Code" that fostered fair competition. In turn the brothers had claimed that the NRA was unlawful, because Congress had improperly delegated too much legislative power to the President. In 1935 on a day New Dealers called "Black Monday," the Court killed the NRA (Schechter Poultry Corp. v. U. S.) and ruled against the Administration in two other important cases. In decisions that followed, the Court continued to strike down Roosevelt's major New Deal legislation.*

LINGERING REMNANT OF NRA: *A "Blue Eagle" poster (below) peels away at the hand of an employee in the Commerce Department, Washington, D. C. Until the Court outlawed the NRA, industries that had voluntarily tried to improve the economy by regulation of production and prices had displayed the "Eagle."*

we operate under approved code and display the Blue Eagle as a symbol of cooperation

FIRESIDE CHAT: *President Roosevelt defends his reorganization plan for the Supreme Court during an informal radio broadcast on March 9, 1937. In this retaliation to the Court's hostility toward his New Deal reform measures, Roosevelt labeled the Court a "third House of the Congress —a super legislature."*

He urged listeners to "save the Constitution from the Court and the Court from itself." His proposal, called "Court-packing" by the public, advocated more Judges, who would bring a "steady and continuing stream of new and younger blood" to the Court.

Again the Supreme Court reviewed a conviction; again Justice Jackson wrote the majority opinion. The trial judge had properly instructed the jury, he said, to decide if Hans Haupt meant only to help his son or if he meant to help Germany against the United States. The jury had found him a traitor, and in law they had sufficient evidence.

"JURORS—PLAIN PEOPLE—have manfully stood up in the defense of liberty" on many occasions, wrote Justice Black in 1955. To deprive 3,000,000 persons of the safeguards in trial by jury went beyond the power of Congress, he declared; a law to do so was unconstitutional, and Miss Audrey M. Toth had won against Donald A. Quarles, Secretary of the Air Force.

Honorably discharged from military service in December, 1952, her brother Robert came home to Pittsburgh and got a job in a steel plant. Air Force police arrested him at work in May, 1953, and flew him to Korea for court-martial on charges of murdering a Korean the previous September.

At Miss Toth's petition, a district court issued a writ of habeas corpus, and the Air Force brought back its prisoner. A court of appeals ruled against him, and then the Supreme Court took the case.

Like Toth, any veteran might be hustled off for court-martial "for any alleged offense" in service, Black warned—if the Court found power for Congress to say so. The Court did not. To provide for justice in such cases, said Black, Congress could give jurisdiction to civilian courts by law.

At an Air Force base in Oxfordshire, England, a sergeant's wife was saying she had killed her husband the night before.

Delusions, thought the Air Force psychiatrist; he knew how she had grown up wretched in a poor and broken home, how her husband squandered money and drank. But he sent men to investigate; they found her husband's body.

Under psychiatric and prenatal care, she waited in a hospital until a court-martial convicted her of premeditated murder and sentenced her to life at hard labor. Flown back to America in 1953, she bore her third child in a federal prison for women.

The Court of Military Appeals ordered a new trial; in 1955 doctors found her sane; then the Supreme Court agreed to hear argument that the Uniform Code of Military Justice denied her constitutional rights to a jury trial under the Sixth Amendment. With her case they took another that raised the same legal issues.

Working under pressure as the term was closing, the Court reached these cases and announced the validity of military trials for civilian dependents abroad. Warren, Black,

CARTOONS PRO AND CON *appeared in news-papers when President Franklin D. Roosevelt tried to add six Justices who would favor his policies. From 1935 until 1937, the Supreme Court pictured below negated New Deal attempts to lift a depressed economy.*

COURTESY JERRY DOYLE

"NINE OLD MEN" OF 1937: *From left are (standing) Owen J. Roberts, Pierce Butler, Harlan Fiske Stone, Benjamin N. Cardozo; (seated) Louis D. Brandeis, Willis J. Van Devanter, Chief Justice Charles Evans Hughes, James C. McReynolds, George Sutherland.*

HARRIS AND EWING

STEEL LABOR

THE VOICE OF THE STEEL WORKERS ORGANIZING COMMITTEE — C.I.O.

MAY 15, 1937   Price Two Cents   43   VOL. II, No. 9

25,000 J & L MEN STRIKE FOR SIGNED CONTRACT

STEEL MILLS TELL SWOC TO CALL STRIKE

Youngstown Sheet & Tube and Republic Workers Demand Contracts

Youngstown, Ohio, May 15.—Delegates of steel union lodges in the Youngstown area have empowered the Steel Workers Organizing Committee, headed by Philip M...... call strikes in .... Sheet t. .....

AN ACT OF BAD FAITH
★ ★ ★ ★   ★ ★ ★ ★

A Statement to the Public on the Steel Crisis, by Philip Murray, Chairman of the Steel Workers Organizing Committee

THERE is a crisis developing on certain "fronts" of the steel industry, as regards management's relations with its workmen, which is of vital interest to the general public. I want the public to know that responsibility for any strike that might take place rests solely with those so-called "big independents" who refuse to give their own workmen the protection they want through a written contract.

To those who might not have been following closely the present successful ....paign of the Steel Workers Organizing Committee, I wish ....ificant fact....... ......eighed in .....de.....

MURRAY CALLS 'WAR' BOARD OF OTHER PLANTS

Jones & Laughlin Refusal to Sign Contract Is Cause of Walkout

Pittsburgh, Pa., May 15.—When Jones & Laughlin Steel Corporation officials refused to sign a SWOC contract 25,000 workmen in Pittsburgh and Aliquippa works of the corporation ...ent on strike. Picket line. .....wn around the mill .....ght and after

AFTERMATH OF A COURT DECISION: *A steel strike in Pittsburgh (right) in May, 1937, followed a Supreme Court case involving Jones & Laughlin Steel Corporation. Its plant in Aliquippa had fired 12 employees who supported the Steel Workers Organizing Committee, a C.I.O. union. When the Court upheld the Wagner Act, which forbids such action by management, it ordered the workers reinstated. The Court's action confirmed labor's right to vote for the union of its choice. But at first the company refused to consent to an election. Workers went on strike and won. Steelworker (below) casts ballot for union preference.*

and Douglas noted dissent; Frankfurter, a "reservation" of opinion.

Then, as it rarely does, the Court granted a petition for rehearing; in 1957 six Justices agreed to reverse the decisions. Congress could not deprive civilians of the safeguards in the Bill of Rights, Black insisted. Under the new ruling, courts-martial may not try mothers, wives, or children of servicemen for crimes carrying a death penalty.

Extending this rule in a series of cases, the Court stopped court-martial trial of dependents for lesser crimes, and of civilian employees abroad for all crimes.

MEANWHILE, in another long series of decisions, the Court was defining the constitutional rules for fair criminal trials in state courts.

Tortured and whipped by deputy sheriffs, three men confessed to murder; in 1936 the Supreme Court found that their state, Mississippi, had denied them due process of law.

Held for days against Indiana law, questioned for hours by relays of policemen, a man named Watts finally said something that convicted him of murder; in 1949 the Court ruled that such coercion also denies due process—if a man's own words may cost his life he must speak at his own choice.

For himself and a codefendant, a man named Griffin wrote a petition: because of their "porverty," they could not pay for a transcript of their trial for armed robbery and without this record they could not appeal in Illinois courts. Griffin thought the Fourteenth Amendment forbade justice "only for 'Rich.'" So did the Justices, in 1956. They ordered Illinois to give Griffin a free transcript; they gave "equal protection of the laws" a new value. If a man with money can buy a hearing because his state offers a right of appeal, that state must help a man without money.

Accused of breaking into a poolroom in Panama City, Florida, in 1961, Clarence Earl Gideon tried to get a court-appointed lawyer, and failed. He tried to defend himself, and failed. He tried to persuade the Supreme Court to review his case, and succeeded. The Court appointed Abe Fortas of Washington to argue Gideon's claim that without a lawyer no man gets the fair trial the Constitution demands.

Before the Justices, Fortas stressed the confusion any layman would feel when Florida said: "Apply the doctrine of *Mapp* v. *Ohio*. Construe this statute of the State of Florida. Cross-examine witnesses. Call your own witnesses. Argue to the jury."

Florida's attorney argued that the issue should be left to the states. But all nine Justices agreed that no man should have to defend himself against a felony charge, trying to apply precedents he never heard of and construe laws he never read. If a defendant has no money for a lawyer, the state court must appoint one for him. On retrial, a Florida jury acquitted Gideon.

As Justice Potter Stewart had pointed out, Florida wouldn't have let Gideon represent anyone else as an advocate in its courts. But as lawyers and newspapers said, in the Supreme Court Gideon could stand for anyone who happened to be poor.

DOLLREE MAPP may stand for anyone who thinks a government should obey its own laws.

To protect the people's right to security, the Fourth Amendment requires federal officers to have specific and detailed warrants for searches and arrests. The states have had similar requirements.

But for many years officers disregarded this. If they broke into a home and seized property contrary to law, prosecutors could use it as evidence in court to convict its owner—government could, and did, break the law to its own advantage.

In 1914 the Supreme Court announced that if federal officers seize things illegally, federal judges must not admit such things in evidence in their courtrooms. But that decision did not bind state courts. Until 1961 the Court left states free to admit such evidence if they chose.

When police arrived at Mrs. Mapp's home in Cleveland, Ohio, on May 23, 1957, she refused to admit them unless they had a warrant. Three hours later they forced a door, handcuffed Mrs. Mapp for being "belligerent," and searched the house thoroughly, hunting for a person "wanted for questioning" and for evidence of gambling. Finding books they thought obscene, they arrested her for having these.

LIKE FATHER LIKE SON AND DAUGHTER, *William and Lillian Gobitas with their father, Walter, between them, believe as Jehovah's Witnesses that saluting the flag is idolatry. Their father charged that compulsory pledges of allegiance to the U.S. flag denied his children freedom of religion, a basic constitutional right. But in 1940 the Court ruled against him.*

HANDS AT HER SIDES, *nine-year-old Jana Gobitas (center) abstains from a present-day flag salute in the third grade classroom of Bayside School, Milwaukee, Wisconsin.*

Unlike her father, William, a fifth grader in the picture taken in 1935 (above right), Jana does not face expulsion from school for bypassing the salute.

In 1943 the Court reversed its ruling in the Gobitas case and said: "Compelling the flag salute . . . and pledge . . . invades . . . the First Amendment to our Constitution," that protects freedom of religion from "all public control."

On trial, Mrs. Mapp offered evidence that a boarder had left the books, some clothes, and no forwarding address. The police did not prove they had ever had any warrant. But Mrs. Mapp got a prison sentence. Ohio's highest court upheld it.

Reviewing *Mapp* v. *Ohio,* the Supreme Court decided in 1961 to bar the doors of every courtroom—state as well as federal—"to evidence secured by official lawlessness." The Fourth Amendment sets standards for search and seizure, said its opinion, and the Fourteenth requires judges to uphold them in every state of the Union. In closing the courtroom doors, the Justices guarded the doors of every home.

TO OPEN all public-school doors to Negro children, without discrimination, the Supreme Court gave its decision in *Brown* v. *Board of Education* on May 17, 1954. Chief Justice Warren read the unanimous opinion: ". . . in the field of public education the doctrine of 'separate but equal' has no place."

Inheriting this doctrine from *Plessy* v. *Ferguson,* the Court first heard full argument on its place in public education in 1938, when the Court ordered Missouri to let a Negro join white students at the state's only law school. By 1951 it had applied the *Plessy* doctrine in three other graduate-school cases.

Oliver Brown of Topeka, Kansas, sued the city school board that year in behalf of his eight-year-old daughter

97

ROUNDUP OF ALIENS *in World War II (below) begins an evacuation of persons of Japanese ancestry from west coast military zones. The government shipped the civilians to detention centers like Owens Valley in California (right). More than 110,000 Japanese-Americans endured bleak camp life; one of them painted the picture above.*

FIGHTER *for civil liberty, Dr. Gordon K. Hirabayashi (right), teaches a class at the University of Alberta in Canada. A college senior in 1942, he refused to obey a military order that required Japanese-Americans to register for evacuation to relocation centers. He claimed that the Army order violated his rights as a U. S. citizen. His plea failed when the Supreme Court (Hirabayashi v. U. S.) held that the threat of invasion and sabotage sanctioned the military restriction of constitutional rights among Japanese-American citizens.*

QUIRIN

KERLING

HEINCK

NEUBAUER

HAUPT

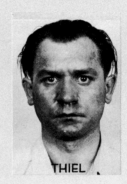
THIEL

EIGHT NAZI SABOTEURS, *foiled by FBI agents in their attempt to cripple U. S. industrial plants in 1942, faced trial by a military commission. Their lawyers, assigned by President Roosevelt, applied to the Supreme Court, claiming the commission was unlawfully appointed. But the Court upheld the commission under the powers of the President and Congress (Ex parte Quirin).*

TOOLS OF DESTRUCTION: *Nazi saboteurs, in teams of four as shown above, landed from U-boats, one team at Long Island, New York, the other south of Jacksonville, Florida. Each team brought ashore boxes of high explosives (below) that included TNT disguised as coal, incendiary pen-and-pencil sets, fuses, detonators, primers, and an assortment of mechanical and chemical timing devices. Coast Guardsmen discovered the New York team's cache buried with German uniforms in sand dunes.*

Linda Carol. She had to cross railroad yards to catch the bus for a Negro school 21 blocks away; her father wanted her in the white school only five blocks from home.

Three federal judges heard testimony on teachers, courses of study, buildings; they heard lawyers for Brown and 12 other Negro parents argue that the Kansas law permitting segregation violated the Fourteenth Amendment. Finding the schools substantially equal, the judges ruled against Brown; they said that *Plessy* controlled the case.

Ten-year-old Harry Briggs, Jr., and 66 other Negro children had filed a similar suit, through their parents, against school authorities in Clarendon County, South Carolina. The county was spending $395,000 for 2,375 white pupils, $282,000 for 6,531 Negro pupils. All the white students had desks; two Negro schools had no desks at all.

Like the other school cases, this was a suit in equity: if someone suffers a wrong and the law provides no remedy, he may ask a court of equity for relief; for centuries such courts have had power to fashion special remedies to serve the ends of justice.

The federal court that heard the *Briggs* case ordered Clarendon County to "equalize" its schools as soon as possible; but,

TWO ESCAPED EXECUTION: *Dasch and Ernest Burger lost courage and exposed the sabotage plot to the FBI. Within 14 days of their landing all the saboteurs had been captured. The two informers were spared the electric chair—the fate of the other six. Below, Maj. Gen. Myron C. Cramer, Judge Advocate General of the War Department, holds shovel used as evidence in trial of the men.*

BURGER   DASCH

GERMAN UNIFORM CAP *crowned the military dress worn by the saboteurs when they landed. Not until they changed into civilian clothes on the beach did the raiders become liable for espionage and the death sentence it carried under the laws of war.*

AIR FORCE POLICEMAN *in Korea, Robert Toth (left) was honorably discharged from the service only to be arrested by the Air Force while working in a Pittsburgh steel plant in 1953. Charged in the death of a Korean civilian who had been shot by an Air Force sentry one night when Toth had been on guard duty, the former airman was flown back to Korea to face a military trial. Toth went free when the Supreme Court held that ex-servicemen may not be tried by court-martial for alleged service crimes (***Toth v. Quarles***). He hugs mother and sister (opposite) on his return to the United States.*

relying on *Plessy,* it refused to order Negro pupils admitted to white schools, or to rule South Carolina's segregation law invalid.

The Supreme Court heard argument in December, 1952, on the *Brown* and the *Briggs* cases, combining them with an almost identical case from Prince Edward County, Virginia, and one from Delaware.

Delaware's court of equity had found separate Negro schools inferior and ordered Negro children transferred to white schools at once; its highest court had sustained the order, and school officials had sought review in the Supreme Court.

Briefs for all the Negro litigants included data from psychologists and social scientists. Since Brandeis filed his famous brief for Oregon in 1908, lawyers had offered "non-legal" facts to defend a challenged law; now they offered such material to attack state laws. Records from the lower courts printed the testimony of expert witnesses explaining why they thought legal segregation harmed Negro children.

The Justices heard attorneys for the Negroes contending that discrimination by race violated the Fourteenth Amendment, and attorneys for the states insisting it did not.

In June, 1953, the Court ordered a reargument, inviting the Attorney General of the United States to take part. If historical evidence could show how Congress and the ratifying states meant the Fourteenth Amendment to affect public schools, the Justices wanted to hear it. They also wanted argument on the Court's own equity powers. They heard it in December.

The Justices found history conclusive on one point: Public education has gained importance and scope since 1868. On other points history was uncertain, the Justices concluded. They ruled that segregation in public schools deprives children of "the equal protection of the laws guaranteed by the Fourteenth Amendment."

The May, 1954, rulings affected 21 states and the District of Columbia. But the Justices did not order specific changes at once. They gave all the states affected a chance to be heard in yet another argument, this one on appropriate remedies.

Some states filed briefs: Oklahoma explained that it would have to rewrite its tax laws; North Carolina and Florida included long reports on public opinion.

On May 31, 1955, the Chief Justice again spoke for a unanimous Court. The cases would go back to the lower courts; these would review the work of local officials facing the problem of unprecedented change.

In the 12 fat volumes of record, the Justices read one plaintiff's testimony. Telling

"why I got into the suit whole soul and body," Silas H. Fleming said, "the only way to reach the light is to start our children together in their infancy and they come up together." And they read the official comment of the State of Florida: "We think the only answer is time and the patient efforts of those who value democracy more than their personal longings and private prejudices."

TAXATION without representation is tyranny, American colonists were saying angrily in the 1760's. In the 1960's, voters in American cities were saying the same thing.

City voters sent some lawmakers to Congress and the state legislatures, of course; but in many states rural voters—a minority of the population—sent more. People had been moving from farms to cities, but electoral districts had not changed.

One Vermont representative spoke for 49 people in 1950, another for 33,155. In Connecticut, a mere 9½ percent of the people could elect a majority of the state's representatives. By 1955, the Colorado legislature was giving Denver $2.3 million a year in school aid for 90,000 children; it was giving a semirural county $2.4 million for 18,000 pupils.

Although the Supreme Court had decided cases on voting frauds and discrimination in state primary elections, it had dismissed a case on Congressional apportionment in 1946. "Courts ought not to enter this political thicket," Justice Frankfurter had warned; federal judges had obeyed.

Nevertheless, Charles W. Baker of Memphis, Tennessee, and nine other qualified voters, filed a suit in equity against Joe C. Carr, Secretary of State, and other officials. They asked a federal court to order changes in the state's election procedure.

The Tennessee constitution said electoral districts should be changed every 10 years so each member of the legislature would represent about the same number of voters. But the General Assembly had not passed a reapportionment law since 1901.

DIVISION OF CORRECTIONS

CORRESPONDENCE REGULATIONS

MAIL WILL NOT BE DELIVERED WHICH DOES NOT CONFORM WITH THESE RULES

No. 1 -- Only 2 letters each week, not to exceed 2 sheets letter-size 8 1/2 x 11" and written *on one side only,* and if ruled paper, do not write between lines. *Your complete name* must be signed at the close of your letter. *Clippings, stamps, letters* from other people, *stationery* or *cash must not be enclosed* in your letters.

No. 2 -- All *letters* must be addressed in the *complete prison name* of the inmate. *Cell number,* where applicable, and *prison number* must be placed in lower left corner of envelope, with your complete name and address in the upper left corner.

No. 3 -- *Do not send any packages without a Package Permit.* Unauthorized *packages* will be destroyed.

No. 4 -- *Letters* must be written in English only.

No. 5 -- *Books, magazines, pamphlets,* and *newspapers* of reputable character will be delivered *only if* mailed direct from the publisher.

No. 6 -- *Money* must be sent in the form of *Postal Money Orders* only, in the inmate's complete prison name and prison number.

INSTITUTION ____________ CELL NUMBER ____________

NAME ____________ NUMBER ____________

In The Supreme Court of The United States
Washington D.C.

clarence Earl Gideon
Petitioner
VS.
H.G. Cochran, Jr, as director, Divisions of corrections State of Florida

Petition for a Writ of Certiorari Directed to The Supreme Court State of Florida.

No. 890 Misc.
OCT. TERM 1961
U. S. Supreme Court

To: The Honorable Earl Warren, Chief Justice of the United States

Comes now the petitioner, Clarence Earl Gideon, a citizen of The United states of America, in proper person, and appearing as his own counsel. Who petitions this Honorable Court for a Writ of Certiorari directed to The Supreme Court of The State of Florida. To review the order and Judgement of the court below denying The petitioner a writ of Habeus Corpus.

Petitioner submits That The Supreme Court of The United States has The authority and jurisdiction to review The final Judgement of The Supreme Court of The State of Florida the highest court of The State Under sec. 344(B) Title 28 U.S.C.A. and Because The "Due process clause" of The

PLEA OF A PAUPER: *Clarence Earl Gideon (far right) signs copies of* Gideon's Trumpet, *the story of a case that heralded new hope for destitute defendants. Charged with breaking into a poolroom, penniless when brought to trial, Gideon asked the court to appoint counsel. But the judge refused, saying that Florida law provided indigent defendants with counsel only if they faced the possibility of the death sentence. Convicted, Gideon spent hours in the prison library consulting law books. Then he penciled the petition (left) asking the Supreme Court to hear his case. The Court appointed attorney Abe Fortas (below) to represent him. In 1963, it decided Gideon had been denied a fair trial, adding that every state must provide counsel to an indigent prisoner charged with a felony* (**Gideon v. Wainwright**). *Later, at a retrial his lawyer won acquittal for Gideon.*

NATIONAL GEOGRAPHIC PHOTOGRAPHER ROBERT F. SISSON

When the lower court dismissed *Baker* v. *Carr,* the Supreme Court accepted it. The Justices studied briefs with maps of voting districts, and a special brief for the United States; they heard argument twice. Then, setting precedents aside, the Court decided that minority rule in state legislatures is a matter for judges to review.

Justice Brennan spoke for the majority. If a state lets one man's vote count for more than another's because they live in different districts, that state denies its citizens equal protection of the laws. Citizens wronged by "debasement of their votes" may go to court for help.

In March, 1962, the Court sent Baker's case back to the district judges for them to decide. By November, voters in 30 of the 50 states were suing in state as well as federal courts for new voting districts.

RICH CLARKSON, TOPEKA CAPITAL-JOURNAL

BARRED BY HER COLOR: *When a white public school turned away Linda Brown (left, today Mrs. Charles D. Smith of Topeka, Kansas), her father contended that segregated public schools lacked "equal" educational opportunities. Such discrimination infringed upon his daughter's constitutional rights, he claimed. The resulting case became the most famous in modern Court history. In 1954, unanimously rejecting the "separate but equal" doctrine of the 1896* **Plessy v. Ferguson** *case, the Court shed new light on the "equal protection of the laws" provision of the Fourteenth Amendment. In public education, the Court concluded: "Separate educational facilities are inherently unequal"* (**Brown v. Board of Education**). *This ruling affected 21 states with segregated schoolrooms such as the one at right. It also spurred a revolution in the legal status of Negroes in all avenues of life. Because of the decision, young Chuckie, on his mother's lap at left, is free to attend a desegregated classroom like the one below.*

LARRY KEIGHLEY (ABOVE) AND WERNER WOLFF, BLACK STAR © N.G.S.

A case from Georgia brought Congressional apportionment before the Court again; it ruled in 1964 that Congressional districts should be equal in population.

Alabama appealed to the Court when district judges rejected three reapportionment plans for the state. Sustaining the lower court, the Justices listed new rules for a state legislature. Both houses must be based on population, they said; and if districts differ in population, the Court would not find the differences valid for geographic, historic, or economic reasons alone.

In these cases Justice Harlan dissented. (President Eisenhower had appointed him in 1955 to the Court his grandfather had served.) Harlan insisted that a state might prefer to give some areas more voice in lawmaking than population alone would warrant, and the Court should respect a state's decision. On Congressional districts, he found no constitutional mandate for courts to take action; and Justice Stewart agreed with him.

"ALMIGHTY GOD, we acknowledge our dependence upon Thee, and we beg Thy blessings upon us, our parents, our teachers and our Country."

As supervisors of the state's public education under New York law, the Board of Regents wrote this classroom prayer in 1951. Formal religion has no place in public schools, they said, but "teaching our children, as set forth in the Declaration of Independence, that Almighty God is their Creator" would give the "best security" in dangerous days. They recommended their prayer to local school boards; some accepted it, including the board in New Hyde Park, which voted in

107

1901

Memphis ●

43,000 VOTERS
7 1/2 REPRESENTATIVES

43,000 VOTERS
11 REPRESENTATIVES

1950

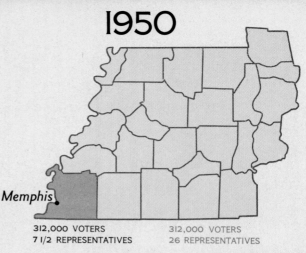

Memphis ●

312,000 VOTERS
7 1/2 REPRESENTATIVES

312,000 VOTERS
26 REPRESENTATIVES

BATTLE OF THE BALLOT: *Unequal voting rights in Tennessee cast a Court case. Maps (above) depict problem. In 1901 eight counties had as many people as Memphis and elected nearly the same number of representatives. By 1950 Memphis' population equalled that of 24 counties. Under the state constitution the city should have gained more representatives, but it did not; so the rural vote counted almost four times more than the urban. Reviewing the city voters' complaint that this denied them equal protection of the laws, the Court in 1962 held that judges should hear and decide such claims under the Fourteenth Amendment (**Baker v. Carr**).*

1958 for the prayer to open each school day.

Some parents objected; they feared that if government may regulate or require any religious practice in a public school it gains power over matters which should be free.

The classroom ceremony offended families who were Jewish, Unitarian, members of the Society for Ethical Culture, and nonbelievers. Steven I. Engel and four other parents asked a New York court to order the prayer discontinued. New York's constitution and the Nation's forbid any "establishment of religion" by law, they insisted.

William J. Vitale, Jr., and other board members replied that the prayer gave moral training for good citizenship. On request, they said, any child would be excused.

By adopting the Regents' prayer, schools did not prefer or teach religion, New York courts held; but schools must not compel any child to pray. In 1961 the Supreme

Court took *Engel* v. *Vitale* for review; it let religious groups and the Regents file special briefs as *amici curiae,* "friends of the court." The briefs outlined the controversy.

For Engel: Americans have been a devout people; but to study their history is one thing, to worship God is another. By composing and instituting a prayer, the 13 Regents—all laymen and state officials—had taken on the work of clergymen. James Madison had denied "that the Civil Magistrate is a competent Judge of Religious truths or that he may employ Religion as an engine of Civil policy. The first is an arrogant pretention . . . the second, an unhallowed perversion of the means of salvation." On these grounds, Engel said, the First Amendment forbids Congress to establish religion, the Fourteenth forbids the states.

For Jewish groups: Prayer can never be "nonsectarian." Differences in its forms

VOTING IN VERMONT: *Since each town in the state elects one representative to the legislature, ballots marked by two voters in a small rural community may count as much as 1,400 votes cast by residents of some cities. This unbalanced voting power reflects today's national problem that plagues the courts, the other branches of government, and all American citizens—minority rule by rural areas. Since the Court's decision in* **Baker v. Carr,** *courts across the Nation have heard lawsuits against rural voting domination.*

and words go to the essence of faith; no governmental official has constitutional power to enter this realm.

For the Regents: As far as separation of church and state permits, schools must be moral and spiritual guides against threats from "an atheistic way of life," from rising delinquency and crime.

For Vitale and the board: Public schools should not have to give up "any recognition —even on a voluntary basis—of the existence of a Divine Being."

For parents agreeing with the board: No group should "force all others to conform to their views" and demand "the total and compulsory elimination of God's name from our schools."

Mr. Justice Black gave the Supreme Court's opinion in June, 1962: a "solemn avowal of divine faith," the Regents' prayer was religious—and unconstitutional, be-

cause the authors of the Constitution thought religion "too personal, too sacred, too holy," for any civil magistrate to sanction. No government should compose official prayers for Americans to recite.

Dissenting, Mr. Justice Stewart thought the decision denied children the chance to share "the spiritual heritage of our Nation."

When lawyers for two other school boards appeared in 1963, they praised the ruling in *Engel* v. *Vitale* but insisted that it did not apply to their cases. In their schools official prayers had no place—pupils read the Holy Bible and recited the Lord's Prayer every day, unless parents wanted them excused.

Professed atheists, Mrs. Madalyn E. Murray of Baltimore and her son William challenged the school exercises for favoring belief over nonbelief. Mr. and Mrs. Edward L. Schempp of Abington, Pennsylvania, wanted to teach their three children

Unitarian beliefs without "contradictory" practices at school. As taxpayers and parents of students, they had standing to sue.

Reviewing these two cases, the Supreme Court declared again that no state may prescribe religious ceremonies in its schools, that the Constitution stands between the official and the altar.

PUBLIC ANGER over the Supreme Court's powers and decisions ran high in Marshall's day and in Taney's. Charles Evans Hughes saw a third great crisis. Once again, in recent years, attacks on the Court have flared and spread.

Controversies like these come when the Nation confronts new difficulties and new dangers. The Justices review a case arising under the Constitution, as citizens all over the country debate the issues it involves. Then the Court must rule on questions affecting—and dividing—the whole people. The people judge the Court's opinion for themselves; inevitably they disagree.

Critics have challenged the Court's rulings on civil liberties and accused it of pampering Communists and criminals. Bitterly and angrily, southerners have denounced its rulings on race and civil rights. Members of Congress and state legislatures have debated constitutional amendments to overrule the Court on reapportionment. Clergymen and laymen have charged that the Court favors godless materialism.

With equal force and passion, other citizens have answered that the Court should decide such cases as these, and insisted that it has decided them rightly.

So the quiet home of the Supreme Court has been the center of a national storm. Almost certainly it will be a storm center in years to come.

UNCONSTITUTIONAL ACT OF FAITH: *Grade-school students begin the day with a prayer. New York residents claimed that when state officials composed a school prayer they trespassed on the religious guarantees of the First Amendment. Emphasizing separation of church and state, the Supreme Court in 1962 outlawed state prayers in public schools (**Engel v. Vitale**).*

WIDE WORLD (BELOW) AND NATIONAL GEOGRAPHIC PHOTOGRAPHER EMORY KRISTOF © N.G.S.

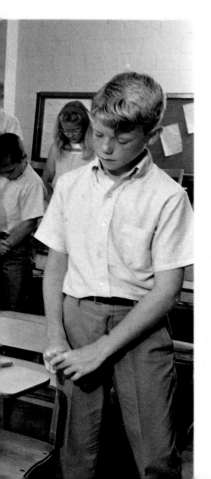

OPPOSED TO BIBLE READING *and recitation of the Lord's Prayer as daily rituals in public schools, Edward Schempp (left) and his family charged that these practices amounted to establishment of religion by the state. In 1963 the Court held both of the religious observances unconstitutional in public schools.*

While the Constitution remains the supreme law of the land, Americans will argue about its checks and balances of power, its guarantees of liberty.

As long as the Supreme Court remains the living voice of the Constitution, it will have to say what the law is. This is "the very essence of judicial duty," by John Marshall's own definition.

Other citizens will have to speak, with the Justices, to defend the principle James Madison proclaimed: "While we assert for ourselves a freedom . . . we cannot deny an equal freedom to those whose minds have not yet yielded to the evidence which has convinced us."

For the Supreme Court alone cannot sustain the heritage of equal justice under law. Although the Court symbolizes the judicial power of the United States in action, it shares its highest duty with everyone who loves liberty. And, as Abraham Lincoln asked in 1861, "Why should there not be a patient confidence in the ultimate justice of the people?"

Before the altar of law, tourists gaze upward as a guide (left aisle) describes the

Within the Court Today

"THE REPUBLIC endures and this is the symbol of its faith." Thus spoke Chief Justice Charles Evans Hughes on October 13, 1932, when he joined President Herbert Hoover in laying the cornerstone of the new Supreme Court Building. At that point in time, his words were freighted with special and somber meaning. Throughout the land there were many

Ionic columns of the Supreme Court Chamber, imposing room where the Justices sit.

who doubted then that the Republic *would* endure. Since 1929 the country had been sinking deeper and deeper into history's greatest depression.

Five months later Hoover handed over the Presidency to Franklin Delano Roosevelt. By October 7, 1935, when the Supreme Court sat for the first time in its new home, the clouds were lifting. The New Deal was

under way, business was recovering, and the army of unemployed was dwindling.

Nations and empires have vanished since then, but the Republic has endured. So has its faith, and so has the Supreme Court. Gleaming bone-white and austere among its distinguished neighbors on Capitol Hill, the Supreme Court Building impresses many viewers as more like a temple of ancient

Greece than the modern seat of the judiciary, "silent arm" of the three-branched United States Government.

When architect Cass Gilbert submitted his design in May, 1929, his aim was "a building of dignity and importance suitable for its use as the permanent home of the Supreme Court of the United States." Gilbert was chosen by a building commission headed by Chief Justice William Howard Taft. Associates were Cass Gilbert, Jr., and John R. Rockart, with executive supervision by David Lynn, Architect of the Capitol.

INTO THE BUILDING the architects put about three million dollars' worth of marble from domestic and foreign quarries. For the exterior walls alone 1,000 carloads of flawless white stone came from Vermont —24,700 blocks and slabs ranging in weight from 200 pounds to 63 tons.

For sculptor James E. Fraser's two allegorical figures flanking the entrance, Vermont quarried a 250-ton slab. Georgia marble was chosen for outer walls of the four courtyards that divide the building into a cross-shaped center core and a surrounding gallery of offices and corridors. Nearly square, the resulting structure towers 92 feet high and stretches 385 feet on its longest side. Interior corridors and walls are faced with Alabama marble.

Opposite the main entrance, at the end of an imposing main hall, stands the Courtroom. Gilbert walled the 82- by 90-foot chamber in "Ivory Vein" marble from Spain. His design for the Courtroom interior called for 24 massive columns to support the ornate ceiling. For these the architect insisted on marble of a particularly delicate tint, a stone called "Silver Gray," or "Light Sienna Old Convent," from the Montarrenti Quarry in Italy. At Gilbert's request, an expert went to the quarry to see if it would be physically possible to remove such huge blocks as the plans called for; he found with relief that it could be done.

From Italy the rough stone went to a firm of marble finishers in Knoxville, Tennessee. They dressed and honed it into 72 slightly tapered cylinders measuring 11 feet in circumference at the widest. Three sections went into each 30-foot column, topped by an Ionic capital of the same material.

Against this rare stone, the red of heavy draperies and the dark luster of solid Honduras mahogany add richness to the room where the Supreme Court holds its sessions.

Not everyone liked the new building— including Associate Justice Harlan Fiske Stone, who later became Chief Justice. At first he called it "almost bombastically pretentious . . . wholly inappropriate for a quiet group of old boys such as the Supreme Court." Among the Court's unsolved mysteries is the identity of the Justice who said he and his brethren would be "nine black beetles in the Temple of Karnak."

Neither Taft nor the architect lived to see their dream building completed. The Chief Justice and former President died in 1930, and Gilbert four years later.

Occupants of the nine judicial suites, or chambers, in this magnificent temple hold positions of unique power, prestige, and responsibility in the federal government.

The President appoints Justices—in effect, for life—with the advice and consent of the Senate. A Justice may be removed only by "Impeachment for, and Conviction of, Treason, Bribery, or other high Crimes and Misdemeanors." Never in the Nation's history has this happened.

Article III of the Constitution provides that Supreme Court Justices, and all other federal judges, hold their offices during

TRIUMPHS OF MANKIND *in the struggle for a just society blazon sliding bronze doors at the Supreme Court entrance. Eight relief panels trace the evolution of law from ancient Greece and Rome to the young United States. Every evening guards push shut the huge doors, which weigh six and one-half tons each. Tortoises (left), symbols of righteousness and longevity, support lamp standards.*

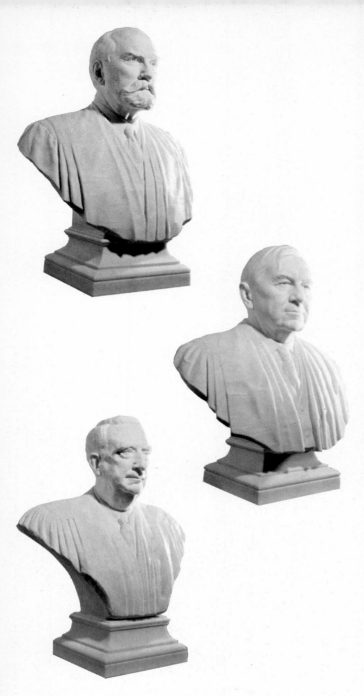

SHRINE AS WELL AS SEAT OF JUSTICE, *the Court's first permanent home commands respect from visitors. Half a million of them pay homage annually. A guard (right) directs a group to the Courtroom door at the rear of the Main Hall. Marble busts of Chief Justices Charles Evans Hughes (top), Harlan Fiske Stone, and Fred M. Vinson stand among the hall's massive columns. These three presided in the present building, completed in 1935. Busts of earlier Chief Justices remain in the old Supreme Court Chamber in the Capitol.*

"good Behaviour." They may, however, resign at any time or retire when eligible. Once a Justice has won Senate confirmation, sworn to uphold the Constitution, donned his robe, and ascended the bench, he enters a world of almost Olympian detachment from the hurly-burly of Washington life.

By the very nature of his position and duties prescribed by law, a Justice stands apart from the pressures and tensions that often make government service a trying experience—the requests from other offi-

cials, the demands from constituents. At the Court the strongest pressure takes a subtle form, felt in the minds or consciences of "fallible human beings," as Associate Justice William J. Brennan, Jr., put it, who live with the awareness "that their best may not be equal to the challenge."

For all their seeming aloofness, however, the Justices remain very much involved in the affairs of everyday life. Each has jurisdiction over one or more of the Nation's 11 judicial circuits. As Circuit Justice he can

decide certain matters which are presented to him alone rather than to the entire Court. In this role he may issue injunctions, grant bail, order stays of execution.

The new building gave the Justices private chambers for the first time in the Court's history. In the old days, they did their opinion-writing and other official work at home. At first they even lacked a robing room, and donned their gowns as they mounted the bench. Now they have a special, handsomely appointed room where they put on their

SEATS OF JUSTICE: *A visitor to the Court sees this view of the bench. The chairs vary in appearance, since each Justice may choose one to suit his personal comfort. The two senior Associates sit on either side of the Chief Justice's chair (center), Justice Black on the visitor's left, Justice Douglas, right. Next to them are Justice Clark, left, Justice Harlan, right, then Justice Brennan, left, Justice Stewart, right. The two junior Associates occupy seats at ends, Justice White, left, Justice Fortas, right.*

119

MARSHAL OF THE COURT, *T. Perry Lippitt is guardian of decorum, paymaster, and business manager. In his office (above), he dresses informally. In the Courtroom he wears cutaway and striped trousers, also the attire of the Clerk of the Court. Lippitt opens each Court session with the traditional chant: "Oyez! Oyez!! Oyez!!!"*

judicial dress before entering the Courtroom.

Today the Justices work in richly carpeted, oak-paneled three-room suites. Each Justice decorates his quarters to his own taste. The newest member of the Court, Associate Justice Abe Fortas, who plays the violin in a string quartet every week, has chosen an autographed black-and-white drawing of his friend Pablo Casals, the great cellist, to hang above his desk.

Objects of art and oddments collected on expeditions to remote corners of the world dominate the decor in Justice William O. Douglas's chambers.

Justice Tom C. Clark, proud of his Texas origin, displays the Lone Star flag together with the official ensign of the Attorney General, a post he held under President Truman. On walls and shelves, plaques and testimonials acknowledge his efforts to improve judicial administration throughout the country.

Among the somber volumes in Justice Byron R. White's chambers nestle two footballs covered with players' autographs— souvenirs of "Whizzer" White's days as halfback with the Detroit Lions and Pittsburgh Pirates (now the Steelers) to earn his way through Yale Law School.

Shortly after Justice White came to the Court in 1962, a law clerk working late heard an odd thumping in the corridor. Opening the door, he saw the then junior Justice dribbling a basketball on his way to the building's third-floor gymnasium.

Cass Gilbert, Jr., suggested the small gym. Although the Justices seldom use it, their law clerks play against the library staff or the Court's police at basketball and paddle-tennis matches.

The Chief Justice's perquisites include larger chambers, three law clerks, an extra secretary or more if need arises, and a government limousine with chauffeur. Associate Justices have two law clerks and a single secretary apiece, and make do with their own automobiles. A messenger rounds out each Justice's personal staff.

About 250 persons go to work daily in the Supreme Court Building. Among them are officers the Court appoints to ensure the proper functioning of its business.

For all professional matters, the Clerk, John F. Davis, and his assistants are the link between the Justices and the legal world outside. He and his staff handle the Court's immense flow of paper work, checking and recording the petitions that arrive by the dozen daily, and preparing an agenda.

The Clerk also receives lawyers' applications for admission to the Supreme Court bar; he schedules the attorneys' introduc-

tions; and after the Chief Justice greets the candidates, the Clerk swears them in as members of the bar. Later, if they have questions on the Court's procedure—when to file appeals, for instance—they consult the Clerk.

As business manager and executive, the Marshal, T. Perry Lippitt, handles payrolls, purchases supplies, and pays the bills. He also directs a police force of 33, escorts visiting dignitaries, and supervises public tours of the building.

WHEN the Justices are not sitting, visitors see the two beautiful spiral staircases as well as the Courtroom and Main Hall. Bronze gates bar the public from corridors leading to the Justices' chambers.

Visitors who want to see the Court in session line up to be admitted as seats become available. First they must check cameras and umbrellas. The Marshal and his

MUCH ADMIRED BUT SELDOM USED *stairs spiral through five floors. Two elliptical staircases, barred to public use, serve as fire escapes. Despite such showpieces, the building cost nearly $94,000 less than the $9,740,000 appropriated for it.*

aides discourage the presence of small children, and courteously turn away men or women in clothing deemed too informal.

Constantly during a session messengers patrol the aisles to see that no one breaks the rules by sketching or taking notes. Occasionally they silence talkers, or remind a member of the bar to button his coat.

The Marshal has jurisdiction over Court pages, whom he appoints with approval of the Chief Justice. The pages, four boys chosen when high school freshmen, attend Capitol Page School with their counterparts from the Senate and House.

When Court is in session, the pages wait alertly on small straight chairs behind the bench. Frequently they leap up to pass written notes from Justice to Justice, or serve glasses of water. They may disappear behind the curtains to deliver messages to a Justice's staff; and one secretary declares, "They always find you!"

For years the pages wore, and disliked, black or dark-blue knickers and black stockings. Now they wear dark suits with long trousers. Formerly, the boys chosen were less than 64 inches in height; but in 1963 the Court had a page who stood six feet tall.

Until 1961 the pages performed a small rite before the Court convened at noon: They put a pair of goose-quill pens, neatly crossed, before each chair at the two counsel tables facing the bench. Now messengers arrange the pens while the pages hurry from school. Many lawyers appear before the Court only once in a lifetime, and they usually take the quills home as souvenirs.

Snuffboxes, once indispensable, vanished long ago. But other anachronisms survive, hidden by the bench—between the Justices' chairs are five dark green china spittoons.

STATELY READING ROOM *of handcarved oak paneling and massive bronze chandeliers surrounds members of the Foundation of the Federal Bar Association, the sponsor of this book. The third floor of the Supreme Court Building houses the library and part of a collection of 200,000 lawbooks and journals for the Justices, Members of Congress, federal government attorneys, and members of the Supreme Court bar. The reading room and foyer display woodcarvings of ancient jurists.*

"... I WILL DEMEAN MYSELF, *as an attorney and counsellor of this court, uprightly, and according to law...." Lawyers admitted to practice before the Court make their pledge on a Bible acquired in 1808. Succeeding Clerks have initialed and dated it. The Clerk administers the oath to new members of the Supreme Court bar during Courtroom ceremonies before the Justices. About 3,000 attorneys take the oath each year. Many do not appear before the Court more than once.*

To see the Court in action, at its dramatic best, one must choose a day when oral arguments are scheduled.

A few minutes before 10 a.m., the Clerk and the Marshal, formally dressed in cutaways, go to their desks below opposite ends of the high mahogany bench. On the dais, pencils, pens, papers, and briefs are waiting at each Justice's place.

Meanwhile, the Justices themselves, summoned by buzzer, don their heavy black garments in the robing room and line up outside the red-velvet curtains.

Promptly at 10, the Marshal brings all the people in the Courtroom to their feet with a whack of his gavel, and announces: "The Honorable, the Chief Justice and the Associate Justices of the Supreme Court of the United States!"

Simultaneously, in a moment charged with drama and majesty, the nine Justices stride through openings in the curtains and move to their chairs. As they and the spectators stand, the Marshal sounds the traditional chant:

"Oyez! Oyez!! Oyez!!!"

WORKING IN STRICT PRIVACY, *Justices rely on Clerk John F. Davis, right, for official contact with the rest of the legal world. Here Mr. Davis confers in his office with Chief Deputy Clerk Edmund P. Cullinan, seated, and Deputy Clerk Michael Rodak, Jr. The Clerk's office receives incoming cases, prepares conference lists for the Justices, and keeps the Court's voluminous records.*

AFFIXING THE SEAL *by rotating the double-knobbed handle, the Assistant Clerk Evelyn Limstrong embosses documents with the official hallmark of the Supreme Court.*

He uses an old Anglo-Norman word, meaning "hear ye," to command silence. He continues: "All persons having business before the Honorable, the Supreme Court of the United States, are admonished to draw near and give their attention, for the Court is now sitting. God save the United States and this Honorable Court!"

The gavel falls again. The Justices and all others take their seats.

Usually, as the first order of business, the Court admits attorneys to its bar — sometimes scores of them, from all parts of the country. The Clerk rises and announces the candidates, singly or in groups. The Chief Justice recognizes the sponsors, who introduce their candidates. After a word of greeting from the Chief Justice, the newcomers take an oath, en masse, from the Clerk.

If an opinion is ready for release, its author announces it. The Chief Justice calls up the first case docketed for argument. As Court and counsel go to work, even the most casual spectator begins to realize that here before him in this solemn chamber, another chapter in the long and stormy epic of American government is being written.

On their high bench the Justices themselves represent the broad spectrum of American life: nine men of widely differing backgrounds and disparate philosophies, bound together in a concept of justice for all.

In the center sits Chief Justice Earl Warren, former Governor of California, champion of civil liberties and spokesman in the historic decision to end segregation in public schools. President Eisenhower appointed him in 1953, after the death of Chief Justice Frederick M. Vinson.

Seniority determines the seating of the other eight members of the Court. At the Chief Justice's immediate right sits the senior Associate, Hugo Lafayette Black, the soft-spoken Alabaman who achieved an outstanding record as a trial lawyer and United States Senator before becoming President Roosevelt's first Supreme Court appointee, in 1937. At the Chief Justice's left sits William Orville Douglas, a 1939 Roosevelt appointee, former professor of law at Yale, once Chairman of the Securities and Exchange Commission, author, explorer, and conservationist.

In descending seniority, these Associates sit to the right of Chief Justice Warren and Justice Black: Tom C. Clark, appointed by President Truman in 1949 after six years of service in the Department of Justice, four as Attorney General; William Joseph Brennan, Jr., formerly a judge of the New Jersey Supreme Court, a Democrat appointed by Republican President Eisenhower in

1956; and Byron Raymond White, former Deputy Attorney General, appointed in 1962 by his World War II comrade in PT-boat operations, President Kennedy.

Flanking Douglas at his left sit Justices John Marshall Harlan, former New York lawyer and prosecutor, appointed by President Eisenhower in 1955; Potter Stewart, former federal circuit court judge in Cin-

VISITING LAWYERS *from many lands learn from Justice William J. Brennan, Jr., (below portrait). In one of the Court's two public conference rooms, he explains the role of the Supreme Court for foreign attorneys attending the Inter-American and Comparative Law Institutes of the New York University School of Law. Other Justices also meet with students and legal groups as work load permits.*

SUPPORTING FORCE *of 250 skilled employees mans the Supreme Court Building. They staff such offices as the press room (upper left), decorated with cartoons about the Court. The press officer passes out news releases to media representatives. On "decision days" reporters jam the ground-floor press room to gather copies of opinions as the Justices announce them in Court.*

In the carpentry shop (upper right) two cabinetmakers work full time to make and repair the Court's furniture. Members of the police force receive assignments (lower right). With the Court as their beat, 32 policemen and one policewoman give visitors directions, politely bar from the Courtroom people too casually dressed, and answer such questions as, "Do the Justices live here?"

Both employees and visitors use the infirmary on the ground floor. Among other facilities, it provides a paraffin bath for the treatment of sprains (above center). Rigid security measures protect the print shop (lower left), where a staff of five workers sets the Court opinions and other official documents in type.

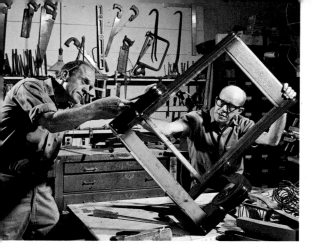

tered his home, where he ran a mail-order business, and seized some of his property.

In clear terms, italicized here, the Fourth Amendment puts limits on searches and seizures: "...no Warrants shall issue, but upon probable cause, supported by Oath or affirmation, and *particularly describing* the place to be searched, and the person or *things to be seized.*"

Stanford's visitors had a warrant to seize material "concerning Communism." A Texas court had issued it on information that he possessed Communist Party literature, membership and dues-payment lists, and other records, in violation of Texas law.

Was this warrant sufficiently specific in describing the place to be searched and the things to be seized? Did it meet the Constitution's requirements? Or was it a "general warrant" like George III's writs of assistance, which goaded Boston patriots toward rebellion in the 1770's?

Stanford's attorney thought the warrant too vague; he asked the Texas court to quash it and return the confiscated property. When the court denied his request, no other state court could consider it. But the Supreme Court granted a petition for review.

When oral argument began, the bearer of a famous Texas name was presenting the petitioner's case against the state—Maury Maverick, Jr., son of the Congressman and grandson of the rancher whose surname became a common noun meaning "unbranded calf." With him was John J. McAvoy of New York. Opposing them were District Attorney James A. Barlow of Bexar County and Hawthorne Phillips, First Assistant Attorney General of Texas.

Maverick reviewed Texas antisubversion law. He argued that it violated provisions in the Bill of Rights and the Fourteenth Amendment. He explained that officers, in a five-hour search, seized Stanford's driver's license, the title to his car, the deed to his house, his health insurance papers, marriage license, and other personal documents.

They also confiscated hundreds of books, pamphlets, and periodicals, said Maverick—including works by Lenin, Eugene Dennis, Erich Fromm, Pope John XXIII's encyclical, *Pacem in Terris,* and "a copy of a dissenting opinion by Justice Hugo Black."

cinnati, Ohio, a 1958 Eisenhower appointee; and Memphis-born Abe Fortas, well known as an appellate advocate and champion of individual liberties, named to the Court in 1965 as President Johnson's first appointee.

Some of the Court's decisions cause nationwide excitement and set off heated controversy. Many more fail to make the front page, but strike home just as effectively.

What happens when a case—spotlighted or little noted—comes before the Court? Take, for example, the case of John W. Stanford, Jr., a bookseller in San Antonio, Texas. State law-enforcement officers en-

United States

"I'LL TAKE THIS *to the Supreme Court!*" *an outraged Bill Smith shouts as he and Charlie Jones argue who was at fault when their automobiles collided.*

But to reach even the first rung of the three-level federal court system, the Smith-Jones quarrel must qualify as a federal case. The Constitution and Acts of Congress prescribe what matters may come before U. S. courts. Others must be tried in state courts.

Should Smith and Jones live in different states, a federal district court can hear their dispute. Juries sit only at this trial level. Either party, if dissatisfied with the decision, may ask review by a court of appeals.

A total of 92 judicial districts in states and territories are grouped into 11 circuits. An appellate bench of three or more judges, depending on work loads, serves each circuit.

Despite his angry promise, Smith probably could take his case no further.

"No litigant is entitled to more than two chances, namely, to the original trial and to a review," Chief Justice William Howard Taft told Congress in 1925. It wrote his view into law with the "Judges' Bill."

To reach the Supreme Court, cases must turn on principles of law, or constitutional questions, that elevate them to far greater significance than the outcome of a specific case, however important it may be to the parties involved.

Of 2,800 or more petitions a year, the highest court in the land selects about 160 on which it hears argument.

Federal courts also review decisions of administrative agencies such as the Tax Court, the Federal Trade Commission, and the National Labor Relations Board.

Congress has provided special, as well as regular, courts. The Court of Claims hears claims against the United States.

The Customs Court decides disputes over duties on imported goods. Its decisions may be appealed to the Court of Customs and Patent Appeals. The latter also reviews judgments of the Tariff Commission and of the Patent Office.

Besides cases from federal courts, the Supreme Court may review decisions of state judges, when cases involve a federal question and every possibility of appeal in the state courts has been exhausted.

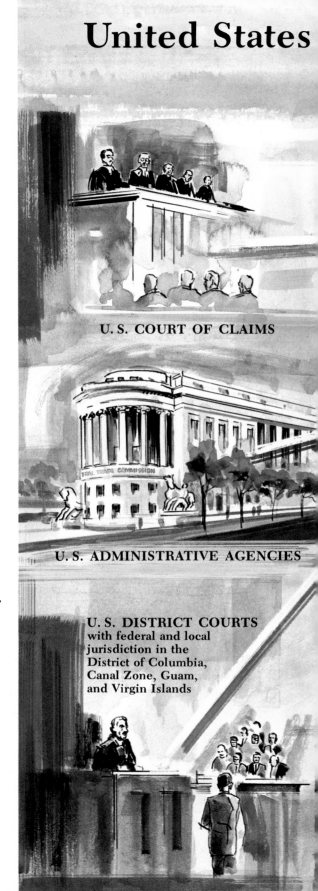

U. S. COURT OF CLAIMS

U. S. ADMINISTRATIVE AGENCIES

U. S. DISTRICT COURTS
with federal and local jurisdiction in the District of Columbia, Canal Zone, Guam, and Virgin Islands

Court System

U.S. SUPREME COURT

U.S. COURT OF APPEALS

U.S. COURT OF CUSTOMS
AND PATENT APPEALS

U.S. DISTRICT COURTS
with federal jurisdiction only
in 50 states and Puerto Rico

APPEALS FROM
STATE COURTS

U.S. CUSTOMS COURT

JUSTICES SURROUND *themselves with objects that reflect their individual tastes and interests. Justice Potter Stewart keeps his grandfather's watch on a mounting that makes it appear like a miniature grandfather clock. Justice William O. Douglas has collected mementos like this Ghanaian carved ivory figurine on his many and varied travels. These treasures reveal the wide range of his expeditions.*

SECLUDED IN HIS CHAMBERS, *Justice Tom C. Clark, here chatting with his law clerks and secretary, Miss Alice O'Donnell, drafts opinions that may alter life for millions. Many certificates lining his walls attest his contributions to the effective administration of justice and his lifelong interest in the Boy Scout movement. For each Justice the Court provides an oak-paneled suite of three rooms and a staff of two law clerks, a secretary, and a messenger. Outstanding young law school graduates, the clerks help conduct the massive research behind each opinion written. The Chief Justice occupies larger chambers. Also, he has three law clerks and additional secretarial aid.*

When he mentioned the last item, a ripple of reaction stirred in the Courtroom. One or two Justices exchanged amused glances. If Justice Black was amused, he did not show it. Expressionless, he sat rocking quietly in his chair beside the Chief Justice.

Justices often question the attorneys. Justice Stewart asked:* Were any of Stanford's personal papers returned to him?

Maverick: They offered to return the marriage license, the deed, the car title, and the insurance papers.

Justice Stewart: When?

Maverick: At the hearing, about ten days

*Excerpts from recorded argument follow.

later. As his attorney, I advised him not to accept them in case this should constitute a waiver.

Justice Stewart: Did they return the dissenting opinion of Mr. Justice Black?

Maverick: No, sir. I have high hopes they will read that opinion and grow in stature.

When Maverick's time expired, District Attorney Barlow took his place at the counsel's lectern. As questions continued, he conceded that no lists of dues payments or other Communist Party records were found in Stanford's home.

Justice White raised issues of freedom of speech and of the press. He asked: If you found a book by Wright Mills [C. Wright Mills, political scientist] on the Communist Party—how would you determine that this book was unlawfully used?

Barlow: I do not know, sir.

Justice White: Why can you seize books? What is unlawful use of such materials? The *New York Times*, the *Washington Post*, the *Washington Star* print news, including reports of decisions here, which might interest the Party. Would this make them objects of seizure?

Barlow: I realize this sounds ridiculous; but they would be, under the state law.

Chief Justice Warren: On what theory did you seize Mr. Justice Black's dissenting opinion?

Barlow: I wasn't in charge of the search, Your Honor. I don't have any theory, sir, on which I can support that.

PHILLIPS followed Barlow, for the State of Texas. Both indicated that Texas authorities would welcome the Supreme Court's answer to questions on the state law's constitutional validity and its possible conflict with federal law.

But characteristically the Court prefers to settle a case on narrow grounds. Just as it refuses to give advisory opinions, it refuses to answer broad constitutional questions not necessary to a decision.

A few weeks after oral argument, the Court handed down its unanimous decision in *Stanford* v. *Texas*. It did not pass on the validity of the state law; it did find that the Texas officers had violated Stanford's constitutional right to be secure in his own home against unlawful search.

In the Court's opinion, Justice Stewart looked to the American Revolution and "those general warrants known as writs of assistance under which officers of the Crown had so bedeviled the colonists." That experience had produced the Bill of Rights.

He said: "The Fourth and Fourteenth Amendments guarantee to John Stanford that no official of the State shall ransack his home and seize his papers under the unbridled authority of a general warrant. . . ."

All opinions go to the Reporter of Decisions, one of the Court's officers, as soon as they are announced. Henry Putzel, with a staff of six, writes headnotes—a short analysis to sum up each opinion. He supervises the publication of *U. S. Reports*, the official record of the Court's work.

A recent example of the variety of subjects the Court considers came in a case that reached literally into millions of American living rooms. It also gave an answer to the question: Who selects those old movies shown on television?

United States v. *Loew's, Inc.*, arose in 1957, when the Department of Justice brought antitrust suits against six major distributing companies that controlled more than 2,000 pre-1948 films.

Testimony in a lower court revealed that each distributor grouped its movies into "blocks," and sometimes refused to make desirable films available to a TV station unless the telecaster took an entire block.

The Justices noted that station WTOP in Washington, D. C., in order to get *Treasure of the Sierra Madre* and four others of equal quality, had to accept such movies as *Nancy Drew, Troubleshooter, Tugboat Annie Sails Again, Kid Nightingale, Gorilla Man*, and *Tear Gas Squad*.

The Supreme Court, agreeing with the court below, held that block-booking of films violated the Sherman Act. As a result of the decision, TV station managements no longer have to buy blocks of films, but may exercise their own taste and judgment in selecting movies to be televised.

Supreme Court cases come in three varieties. Most common are those seeking review of the decisions of federal appellate courts or district courts. The United States has 11 courts of appeals and 88 district courts.

WHERE JUSTICES MEET IN SECRECY: *A messenger prepares the conference room where the Justices meet on Fridays during the Court term to determine what cases to review and what decisions to hand down in cases already heard. So confidential are the conferences that the junior Associate Justice takes incoming messages at the door. On back of each chair a metal plate carries a Justice's name. Chair in foreground belongs to Chief Justice Earl Warren; it faces the seat of senior Associate Justice Hugo L. Black, under portrait of John Marshall.*

JOSEPH J. SCHERSCHEL AND ARLAN R. WIKER © N.G.S.

DONNING ROBE OF OFFICE, *Earl Warren, the Nation's 14th Chief Justice, follows a judicial tradition inherited from England and honored since colonial days. Messenger Hansford Harrison aids the Chief Justice. The Court always selects a messenger taller than the jurists to help them with their robes.*

The next most common case comes from a state court. If any state tribunal decides a federal question and the litigant has exhausted his remedies within the state, then the Supreme Court may consider it.

Last are the "original jurisdiction" actions, brought by one state against another, or between states and the federal government. The Constitution empowers the Supreme Court to hear "all Cases affecting Ambassadors, other public Ministers and Consuls, and those in which a State shall be Party." In such cases the Court sits as a trial body from which there is no appeal.

Most cases reach the Supreme Court when it grants petitions for writs of certiorari. Certiorari, from the Latin *certiorari volumus,* means "we wish to be informed." In effect, it means "send the case to us."

In a recent address Justice Brennan shed light on the Court's way of dealing with its heavy work load. In 1956, when he first came to its bench, he said, litigants sought review in 1,600 cases. Seven years later the total was 2,800, an increase of 75 percent.

"Obviously," he pointed out, "this volume will have doubled before I complete ten years of service. How is it possible to manage such a huge volume of cases? The answer is that we have the authority to screen the cases and select for argument and decision only those which, in our judgment, raise the most important and far reaching questions. By that device we select annually some six to seven percent of the total—in number between 150 and 170 cases—for decision."

The Supreme Court, he explained, does

its screening in a conference room whose proceedings may well be the most secret in a city with many secrets. Here, on Fridays during Court term, the Justices gather in day-long deliberation, discussion, and voting. No one else may enter the room during conference. If a message arrives, the junior Associate Justice takes it at the door.

Five minutes before 10 a.m., on conference days, a buzzer sounds in all the chambers to summon the Justices. Entering the room, they all shake hands even though they may have chatted with each other only a few minutes earlier. They follow this custom whenever they meet. Chief Justice Fuller originated the handshake tradition as a symbol that "harmony of aims if not of views is the Court's guiding principle."

Then the Justices get down to business. Chief Justice Warren sits at the south end of a long table and Justice Black, the senior Associate, at the north end. Along the sides sit the other Justices.

Before him each Justice has a copy of the day's agenda, listing petitions for review and other matters. On it he may have noted his tentative views.

The Chief Justice begins the discussion of each case. He then yields to the senior Associate and discussion passes down the line. After discussion comes the voting, in reverse order of seniority; the junior Associate casts his ballot first and the Chief Justice last. To win review, a case must receive at least four votes.

If it does, counsel submit their briefs and records so each Justice may receive a set two or three weeks before oral argument. Then each party is usually allowed one hour to present his case. Often the Justices have made bench memoranda which they consult while they listen to counsel. These memoranda digest the facts and arguments of both sides, and highlight points about which the Justices may wish to question the lawyers.

The Court follows a schedule of two weeks of Monday-through-Thursday argument, then two weeks of recess for writing opinions and studying petitions for review. On Fridays after argument, the argued cases come before the Justices in their secluded conference room. Here the procedure follows the same pattern as action on petitions, but with much more extended discussion.

Several days after discussion ends and a vote is taken, an opinion is assigned for writing. If the Chief Justice has voted with the majority, he makes the assignment. If

ALERT PAGES *(left to right) Russell Brickell, Frazer Walton, Ernest J. Wilson III (foreground), and Robert Dibble tackle homework while the Court recesses. During sessions they wait behind the bench to relay notes between Justices, serve them glasses of water, and fetch lawbooks. Appointed by the Court's Marshal and the Chief Justice, pages normally begin serving when they are high school freshmen. They and their counterparts in Congress attend the Capitol Page School in the Library of Congress.*

not, the senior Justice of the majority assigns the opinion. The dissenters agree among themselves who shall set down their viewpoint. Even without an assignment, a Justice may write his own opinion, concurring or dissenting.

Law clerks working for the Justices comb every possible source for useful material. These young men come to the Court as honor graduates of the leading law schools, usually upon the recommendation of a dean or professor.

Appointment as a law clerk is regarded as a great stride toward success in a demanding profession. The roster of those who have served the Justices is long and distinguished.

The youngest member of the present

Court, Justice White, served as law clerk to the late Chief Justice Vinson. Dean Acheson came out of Harvard Law School to work for Justice Louis D. Brandeis, later became Undersecretary of the Treasury, then Secretary of State, and now practices law in Washington. Among Justice Oliver Wendell Holmes's clerks—then called secretaries—were Francis Biddle (Harvard Law School '11), who became President Roosevelt's Attorney General, and Thomas G. Corcoran, also Harvard-trained, who won fame as a Roosevelt "Brain Truster," and now heads a large Washington law firm.

Writing an opinion means long, lonely hours of hard work for most Justices. As they call for legal or historical references,

JUSTICES *of the Supreme Court today, these nine members complete a list of 95 Judges who have served since 1790. From left, seated: Associate Justices Tom C. Clark, Hugo L. Black; Chief Justice Earl Warren; Justices William O. Douglas, John M. Harlan. Standing, from left: Associate Justices Byron R. White, William J. Brennan, Jr., Potter Stewart and Abe Fortas.*

Chosen by the President and confirmed by the Senate, the Justices hold office during "good Behaviour" —for life or until retirement.

the lower reaches of this 1,450-mile river. In 1934 the Governor of Arizona sent a scowload of National Guardsmen up the river to halt construction of a dam that would divert water to Los Angeles.

After three unsuccessful Supreme Court suits against California in the thirties, Arizona tried again in 1952. This time the Court appointed a special master, George I. Haight of Chicago, to take evidence and make recommendations. Haight died in 1955; his successor was Simon H. Rifkind of New York City. From 1956 to 1958, Rifkind heard 106 witnesses and received the testimony of 234 more in written depositions.

they have the help of H. Charles Hallam, Jr., librarian and officer of the Court, and his staff of 15. These experts quickly produce the material needed from the library's rich collection, which serves not only the Justices but also members of the bar of the Court, Members of Congress, and law officers of the government.

One of the most formidable cases to confront the Supreme Court provides an example of material that the library has accumulated. This was the battle of the Colorado River, an original-jurisdiction dispute among several western states, particularly Arizona and California.

Since the early 1900's these states had been wrangling over division of waters from

The completed trial record ran to more than 26,000 pages. Briefs and other documents filed by the states took about 4,000 more pages; some six million words were before Rifkind as he wrote his 135,000-word report. It went to the Court in January, 1961. The Justices heard 16 hours of oral argument in the fall of 1961 and six hours more the following November.

Six months later, after reviewing this awesome outpouring, the Court handed down a seven-to-one decision that favored Arizona by denying California any more water than it had been getting under quotas set by Congress in 1928. (Chief Justice Warren, having been Governor of California, did not participate.)

WIVES OF THE JUSTICES *visit at a fountain of Georgia marble in one of the four courtyards. From left: Mrs. Harlan, Mrs. Warren, Mrs. Brennan, Mrs. Black, Mrs. Clark, Mrs. Fortas, Mrs. Stewart, and Mrs. White. When the "Court Ladies," as the press calls them, attend sessions they sit on reserved benches. One of the proudest moments in the life of a Justice's wife, comes when her husband announces his first opinion.*

The Court's opinion was the product of many days and nights of toil by Justice Black. A comparable amount of work went into Justice Douglas's dissenting opinion.

When the author of an opinion feels he has an "unanswerable document," he sends it to the print shop, which operates under rigid security restrictions on the Supreme Court's ground floor. From conference decision to final draft, the Court's findings are carefully

guarded. All parties to a case have a right to learn the decision at the same time, from an official announcement. Moreover, a leak might upset the stock market and even the economy of the country.

Often, after receiving proofs from the print shop, the author finds that his work has only begun. He may revise his draft several times before he circulates copies to his eight brethren.

Then he waits to learn whether those who voted with him still agree, and what they say about his proposed opinion. As Justice Brennan once put it, "often some who voted with him at conference will advise that they reserve final judgment pending circulation of the dissent. It is common experience that dissents change votes, even enough votes to become the majority."

Constantly the Justices exchange comments, in memoranda or at the lunch table. To discuss ideas and wording in complete privacy, they use a special telephone "opinion line" that does not go through the switchboard. A Justice may revise his draft as many as ten times before it wins final approval as the opinion of the Court.

Once all corrections and revisions are in hand, a master proof goes back to the shop for printing. On the day of their release, final copies go to the Clerk of the Court for safekeeping. Several dozen copies also go to the Court's press officer, Bert Whittington, who also puts them under lock and key.

In Court, the author of the majority opinion announces the decision; he may even read the entire opinion aloud. Authors of concurrences and dissents follow suit.

As soon as a decision is announced, the Clerk slips a copy of the opinion into a pneumatic tube that whisks it to the ground-floor press room. There the press officer hands out copies to waiting reporters.

At six desks before the bench in the Courtroom are other men and women from the wire services and major newspapers. They hurry the news by pneumatic tube to colleagues huddled with Teletype machines and telephones in tiny cubicles directly under the bench.

Thus, within minutes the world gets the news of Supreme Court decisions that have been months in the making. Months? Count it figuratively in years, back to the days when the authors of our Constitution dared to build a government for the future. In that bold new experiment, they provided a court system designed to safeguard the rights of every individual—a system that, as the great Chief Justice, John Marshall, said "comes home in its effects to every man's fireside: it passes on his property, his reputation, his life, his all."

Index

PRINTED BY FAW̶
CORPORATION, ROC̶
COLOR PLATES BY LA̶
COMPANY, ALEXAND̶

WILLIAM B. WOODS
1881-87

STANLEY MATTHEWS
1881-89

HORACE GRAY
1882-1902

SAMUEL BLATCHFORD
1882-93

LUCIUS Q. C. LAMAR
1888-93

EDWARD D. WHITE°
1894-1921

RUFUS W. PECKHAM
1896-1909

JOSEPH McKENNA
1898-1925

OLIVER W. HOLMES
1902-32

WILLIAM RUFUS DAY
1903-22

MAHLON PITNEY
1912-22

JAM

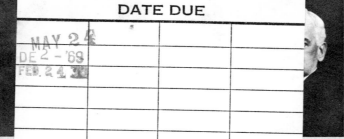

LARKE

WILLIAM H. TAFT°
1921-30

BENJAMIN N. CARDOZO
1932-38

KFURTER
62

WILLIAM O. DOUGLAS
1939-

K M. VINSON°
6-53

TOM C. CLARK
1949-

SHERMAN MINTON
1949-56

EARL WARREN°
1953-

JOHN M. HARLAN
1955-